LIFE LESSONS FROM CRICKET

Life Lessons from Cricket

ADVANCE PRAISE

"Cricket is not only a game which provides us entertainment but it's also a great teacher which depicts what life is all about. Life lessons from cricket is one such fantastic book which allows us to dive deep into elements of building the qualities which makes us live a fulfilling life. I thoroughly enjoyed the experience of reading this book and I hope everyone will feel the same."

—VVS LAXMAN, former Indian cricketer

"A captivating blend of cricket's thrilling moments and life's profound lessons. Life Lessons from Cricket evokes nostalgia and imparts wisdom. Its inspiring traits will resonate with cricket lovers and life enthusiasts alike, encouraging them to play their own game of life with passion and purpose."

**—ARUN DHUMAL, Chairman,
Indian Premier League (IPL)**

"To achieve success, it is crucial to focus on several key qualities: self-discipline, resilience, grit, effective relationship management, and the establishment of trust. In Life Lessons from Cricket, Vimal Kumar and Ashish Ambasta provide a compelling narrative that serves as an invaluable guide for anyone eager to craft a meaningful and impactful life."

—SANJAY SINGH, CEO, Gennova Biopharmaceuticals

LIFE LESSONS FROM CRICKET

BUILDING 20 QUALITIES FOR A SUCCESSFUL LIFE

VIMAL KUMAR & ASHISH AMBASTA

JAICO PUBLISHING HOUSE

Ahmedabad Bangalore Chennai
Delhi Hyderabad Kolkata Mumbai

Published by Jaico Publishing House
A-2 Jash Chambers, 7-A Sir Phirozshah Mehta Road
Fort, Mumbai - 400 001
jaicopub@jaicobooks.com
www.jaicobooks.com

LIFE LESSONS FROM CRICKET
ISBN 978-93-48098-49-8

First Jaico Impression: 2025

Page design and layout by R. Ajith Kumar, Delhi

Contents

Foreword

Cricket has always been more than just a game to me. It has been my greatest teacher, shaping my character and providing me with lessons that have guided me through life, both on and off the field. It is a sport that reveals truths about resilience, leadership, teamwork, and the value of integrity. In *Life Lessons from Cricket*, Vimal Kumar and Ashish Ambasta have beautifully captured the profound parallels between cricket and life. Their work resonates deeply with me, as it articulates the very truths I've lived and learned through this extraordinary sport.

From my earliest memories on the cricket pitch, I've come to understand that the game is a microcosm of life itself. Cricket teaches you how to adapt to changing conditions, handle the pressure of expectation, and recover from setbacks with quiet determination. It demonstrates the importance of preparation, the ability to seize opportunities, and the need to put the team above yourself. Through the chapters of this book, Kumar and Ambasta bring these lessons vividly to life, showing readers how the principles of cricket can illuminate the path to personal and professional growth.

What makes this book particularly impactful is the way it connects cricket's timeless lessons to universal human experiences. Each chapter draws on iconic cricketing moments and lesser-known tales, weaving them into meaningful insights about leadership, ethics, mental strength, and adaptability. By doing so, the authors not only celebrate the beauty of the game but also invite readers from all walks of life to discover its relevance to their own challenges and aspirations.

I found the discussions on leadership especially compelling. Whether it's MS Dhoni's calm under pressure, Sourav Ganguly's fierce determination, or Kapil Dev's inspiring resilience, the examples in this book showcase the many ways leadership can manifest. Cricket has taught me that leadership is not about dominance but about empowerment—about lifting those around you and finding strength in the collective effort. This lesson, central to the game and to life, is explored here with depth and clarity.

The authors also delve into one of the sport's most valuable lessons: how to deal with failure. Cricket is a game of uncertainties, and every player—no matter how great—has faced moments of despair. The stories of legends like Sachin Tendulkar and Rahul Dravid overcoming challenges remind us that setbacks are not the end of the journey but opportunities for growth. It is a lesson I have learned time and again, one that has sustained me during life's inevitable rough patches.

Equally important is the book's emphasis on ethics and fair play, a cornerstone of cricket's enduring appeal. The authors remind us that the spirit of the game is about more than winning—it is about doing so with honour and integrity. Upholding these values is not always easy, but it is what earns respect, both on the field and in life. For me, the moments of greatest pride in cricket have often come not from victory but from acts of fairness and sportsmanship, and this book captures that spirit wonderfully.

Kumar and Ambasta write with a passion and clarity that make this book a joy to read. Their anecdotes, drawn from cricketing history and personal insights, are both entertaining and enlightening. Even those who are not avid cricket fans will find these lessons relevant, as they transcend the game itself. The authors have managed to distil the essence of cricket into a guide for life, offering something valuable for every reader.

As someone who has experienced first-hand the ways cricket can shape a life, I feel a deep connection to the themes explored in this book. Cricket has taught me resilience in adversity, humility in success, and the value of preparation and teamwork. These are the very principles that Kumar and Ambasta so eloquently celebrate in this work.

Life Lessons from Cricket is more than just a book for cricket lovers—it is a book for anyone seeking inspiration and guidance. It is a celebration of the game's power to teach us, to inspire us, and to help us grow. Vimal Kumar and Ashish Ambasta have done a magnificent job in crafting a book that is as engaging as it is thought-provoking. Their insights are a testament to cricket's unique ability to mirror life and to the enduring wisdom it offers to those who play, watch, or simply admire it.

For those embarking on this journey through the pages of this book, I encourage you to embrace its lessons and reflect on how they resonate with your own experiences. Cricket, as I have learned, is not just about results—it's about the process, the moments of courage, and the stories that shape us. This book captures those stories and distils them into something truly meaningful. My congratulations to the authors for this fine achievement—a book that will leave a lasting impact on its readers.

Gregory Stephen Chappell
Former Australian Captain and Cricketer

Preface

Congratulations, Vimal and Ashish, for penning the wisdom shared in this book. While some may dismiss sport as a trivial pursuit, it remains one of the most powerful mediums for building character—or, in those defining moments of a game or career, for revealing it. I firmly believe that, next to health, our character is one of our greatest assets.

I'm often asked who the best cricketer is that I've coached. Having worked with many of the greatest players of the past three decades, I could name plenty. But my answer always remains the same: I am not impressed by talent. Talent is not an accomplishment; it is a gift—bestowed upon us at birth, whether by our parents or a Higher Power. It is something to be grateful for, but it does not define greatness.

What truly impresses me are the athletes who dedicate their time, discipline, and effort to transform talent into meaningful results. And yet, even this so-called "sporting success" falls short.

What's most remarkable is when a highly accomplished athlete is also an exceptional human being. These individuals not only commit to honing their craft but also prioritize becoming the best version of themselves. They lead by example on the field through their skill, dedication, and discipline, and off the field through their humanity. For me, these are the athletes truly deserving of being called "great."

Lance Armstrong may have been one of the most accomplished cyclists, but his cheating and dishonesty disqualify him from true greatness. On the other hand, Indian cricketer Rahul Dravid, while not the fastest or highest run-scorer, exemplifies greatness. His integrity and humility—both during and beyond his playing career—make him a true role model. So much so, in fact, that his humility would likely make him uncomfortable with such a title.

Few are born with the talent to become a great cricketer or athlete. But almost all of us are born with the ability to be a genuinely good human being. We have all the tools to develop sound character, live by a clear set of values and ethics, and contribute meaningfully to the team we call the human race.

Great athletes dedicate immense time to developing their skills—whether batting, bowling, running, jumping, swimming, or otherwise. Yet they also commit themselves to building a solid foundation of character. They embark on a journey of personal mastery, balancing self-focus with genuine care for others. They are as impressive in the public eye as they are in private moments when no one is watching. You see their greatness in their quiet acts of empathy—like showing kindness to a janitor, a security guard, or a fan in worn-out clothing when there are no cameras around.

Too often, fame blinds athletes, celebrities, business leaders, and politicians. Fans, too, are captivated by stellar performances, forgetting that success, money, and fame are fleeting. What endures is the impact of the kind of person we are while we pursue these achievements.

This book provides a powerful framework for navigating life's journey. Using sporting anecdotes, it illustrates how we can better manage ourselves, our relationships, our teams, and the inevitable changes we face.

Ultimately, it's not whether we succeed or fail—both are temporary milestones in the long journey of sport and life. What matters more is how we conduct ourselves while we play the game.

Paddy Upton
South African coach and mental fitness trainer

Introduction

While sports may be considered a trivial pursuit in the larger context of our lives, they act as a great source of happiness. In India, the men's national cricket team, in particular, enjoys tremendous popularity. Their achievements are celebrated with great fervour and pride.

In July 2024, when India men's national cricket team captain Rohit Sharma and his teammates returned from the West Indies after winning the ICC Men's T20 World Cup, they received a delirious welcome with a victory parade in Mumbai. The frenzy of the parade eclipsed even the historic victory procession in 2007, when India had won the inaugural edition of the ICC Men's T20 World Cup.

Indian cricket is indeed replete with fascinating tales and remarkable individuals. This books seeks to explore these stories and highlight the ways in which they can inspire all of us.

It is no secret that, as human beings, we all want to be happy. We constantly act in ways that seek to maximize happiness for ourselves. However, there is a gap between what people believe will give them happiness and what happens when they pursue those things. Often, we err in our judgment.

Psychologists often talk about the concept of cognitive

dissonance, or the mental discomfort people feel when they hold beliefs that contradict one another. Such cognitive dissonance can sometimes lead people to change either their beliefs or their actions. Let us take the example of money. A lot of people believe that earning more and more money alone will make them happy. They work too hard to earn large amounts of money, only to realize that money alone does not have the power to provide true happiness. Rather, the things that give us happiness are our relationships and achievements, and working on something meaningful in life. However, this analysis is limited to external elements. All of us must also reflect on internal elements that allow us to lead a fulfilling life. What are the thoughts and behavioural patterns that one should adopt to experience happiness in the truest sense?

We believe that it is the character of a person which ultimately has a lot of influence on the way the person experiences happiness. People of strong character may endure pain in the short term in order to experience a higher level of happiness in the long term. On the other hand, people of weak character may seek happiness in the short term, but suffer in the long run.

Unfortunately, this is something that is not taught anywhere. You character is, to some extent, built into your DNA, and is also shaped by your surroundings and life experiences—a combination of nature and nurture. Since there is no formal or linear way to explain this topic, we decided to elucidate on character-building in a way that would resonate with readers.

While people watch cricket for its entertainment value, it is also possible to look at the spectacle from a totally different perspective. We can lean into stories from the cricket field and delve into the lessons they provide us. Many life lessons can be learned with a keen eye on the ground. This is exactly what we have attempted to do as the authors of this book.

We come from backgrounds that are similar in some ways and very different in other. Vimal Kumar has spent his career covering the game in all parts of the world for over a quarter of a century as a seasoned journalist, writer, and author. Ashish Ambasta has worked as an HR consultant, gaining insight into organizational cultures and leadership.

The lessons that we learned in our respective careers can seamlessly be applied in other fields as well. In the course of our work, we have seen the difference a person's character makes in bringing positive changes and, thereby, happiness to one's daily life.

All development starts with managing and nurturing the self, which is what the first part of our book focuses on. The first and foremost victory one needs to achieve is the victory over oneself. Before we lead others, we need to lead ourselves. How we handle ourselves in different situations makes us who we are. Many situations test us and help us develop our character through the way we respond to them.

We begin with explaining the concept of hope and positivity as core characteristics of people who bring change into the world. Such people, with their positive outlook and hope in their hearts, inspire others to believe that change is possible and necessary.

Positivity is also the genesis of the second quality of great people—hope.

To understand hope, we need to understand what hopelessness is. When everything is going against you and you know that despite your efforts, it will be difficult to bring about the change you want, you tend to give up. You feel hopeless.

But if you are a hopeful person, such a situation brings out the best in you.

In the cricketing world, there are numerous examples where individual cricketers, as well as teams, were on the verge of being wiped out, but they did not give up and chose to fight back. Learning how to cultivate hope in life in such circumstances is the core of what we have put together in chapter two.

Of course, there are times when you don't get the results you want despite your best efforts. Such situations can weigh you down heavily. But true leaders never give up, which is the essence of resilience. The ability to bounce back from the depths of failure defines a true leader.

Later in the book, we also discuss the concept of discipline, which is what pushes a person to continue doing what needs to be done despite all the temptations in life. Discipline plays a very important role in building character.

Lastly, in this section, we have also explored the concept of grit—the determination to put failures behind and not give up despite the enormity of the challenges. These five elements—hope, positivity, resilience, discipline, and grit—determine a person's control over the self. They build the foundation for becoming a great leader.

Once a person has won over the self, the next step in building a leadership character is to be able to manage relationships and teams. Another reason why nurturing relationships, or team-building, is important is that no one can achieve greatness on their own. For dreams to become reality, one needs the support of others at every stage. There are people who nurture you and help you grow, and then there are those who teach you lessons that can be used to achieve goals. People achieve great things as part of teams that help remove any obstacles from their path.

To build great relationships, we need to begin by being empathetic. We need to put ourselves in the shoes of others and feel the way others feel. When we empathize with others, it opens a window to connect with them. Having empathy also shows that we are not self-centered, and that we listen to others' opinions. It indicates a willingness to collaborate.

The cricketing world is replete with stories of players displaying empathy. Be it English all-rounder Andrew Flintoff providing solace to Australian players after defeating them, or New Zealander Kane Williamson's hug to top oder Indian batter Virat Kohli after the Kiwis won the first World Test Championship final in London in 2021, these are some heartwarming examples of empathy shown by top cricketers. However, along with empathy, one also needs to cultivate emotional intelligence, which offers a unique approach in connecting with others.

The sporting arena is generally charged with emotions, with players passionate to emerge victorious. Despite this, there are ways in which they can practice emotional intelligence to not only manage their own feelings but also tune into others' emotions, whether those of teammates or opposition players. A heightened awareness of others' emotions provides the impetus to build leadership.

Being emphatic and emotionally intelligent boils down to the ability to foster trust. Trust is the glue that binds people together. If one can provide timely help to someone even when they have not asked for it, it helps create trust. In our chapter on trust, we delve deeper into the question of how some leaders can build this trust and achieve results.

Once leaders are able to win the confidence of others and build trust, they must dream big. They must have the courage not only to dream big but also to convince everyone else that the goal in front of them is not unachievable. This courage to challenge the status quo is the hallmark of great leaders. Who can forget the New Zealand team led by Martin Crowe in the 1992 Cricket World Cup, which created a template of sorts of aggressive batsmanship? In 1996, the Sri Lankan team under Arjuna Ranatunga's captaincy displayed immense courage to hit boundaries and sixes from the word go, an unconventional tactic in those days. These are examples of courageous leaders who back their instincts, trust the ability of their team members, and go for the impossible.

People's characters are not defined by victory or defeat, but by the way they react to it. The ability to maintain humility in both victory and defeat goes a long way towards defining a person's character and values. It also endears people to others, and help connect with others more deeply. Humility is the highest form of maturity where we understand that our wins are not ours alone, but are made possible by several factors, some of which are not in our control.

In cricket, one can't control the field and weather conditions or the outcome of the toss, both of which can impact the game. So, it is important to be humble and accept everything with gratitude. This mindset of gratitude leads people to lead more fulfilling lives and to connect with others better.

Once these changes to one's mindset are achieved, the focus needs to shift towards achieving something bigger and better in life. There needs to be a worthy goal, where the person seeks to bring about a change in both their internal and external worlds. This is where one's ability to build and manage a team comes into the picture. In this third section of the book, we have delved into the nuances of building a team and directing it towards achieving greater heights.

The process of building a team starts with a vision, where someone is able to see opportunities much before anyone else, and assembles a team to grab those opportunities. Every single achievement started with a vision, be it the creation of the Indian Premier League (IPL) as a tournament, or the leadership skills of Australian legend Shane Warne, under whom the Rajasthan Royals won the inaugural trophy in 2008.

Vision is the hallmark of a leader, and this vision acts as a goalpost that allows everyone to direct their energies towards achieving the same. But history has taught us that merely having a vision is not enough; it needs to be backed by good judgment, which is nothing but one's ability to foresee challenges, find practical solutions, and look for solutions in the face of difficulties.

A person's ability to judge a situation, assess a person, and understand the context before taking any action defines their success. Action without judgment is similar to hara-kiri (ritualistic suicide practiced by old Japanese samurais), and judgment without action is mere intellectual indulgence. What is required is a combination of both so that one is able to ascertain what needs to be done in pursuit of a vision while also having clarity about the actions required to achieve it.

Having vision and judgment is not enough. Sometimes, even the best laid plans go awry, and one can't do much about it. Even though much care was taken at the beginning and during the implementation of a task, things sometimes don't go as per the plan and that's where perseverance comes in. It's about one's ability to be positive even in the face of difficulties and not lose confidence. It means not giving up despite rejections and failures. One important point to note is that they all played as a team. Each one of them wanted to win and was ready to give everything to the game. In the final analysis, they were hungrier and determined. That their captain Rohit Sharma led them with a lot of guile and wisdom was evident, but, at the end of the day, the team needs to show its character and deliver when it matters. That's where a leader's ability to foster teamwork becomes so important.

But then again, if you lose despite giving it your all, it needs to be handled with a lot of prudence. Who thought India will lose a 50-over World Cup in 2023, which was played on the home ground? Everything was going well for India and Indian team. They were performing well. Batting was clicking, bowling was sharp, their captain was making every decision count, and the coach was doing his job perfectly. The result was evident—they won all their matches right from the beginning until the finals.

And then, in the finals, the Indian team was humbled. There was a lot of despair and disappointment. Fans and the public were shocked, and no one knew how to react. The coach then held the press conference and displayed a lot of prudence by accepting the reality of their defeat in the World Cup finals. He continued sounding hopeful and said that since the process the team adopted was good, it would not be long before they start winning again. This is exactly what happened a few months later in the T20 World Cup when India emerged victorious. This is prudence. This is what defines a person's long-term success and happiness, and that's why it needs to be cultivated.

So far, we have discussed managing self, managing others, and managing teams to achieve what we desire and to be happier. However, there are times when things don't go according to plan. Our best-laid plans are washed away in the storm of uncertainty. We are presented with situations that no one had foreseen, and such situations have become normal. We are truly in a VUCA (Volatility, Uncertainty, Complexity and Ambiguity) world, and we need to adjust to the vagaries of this uncertainty. While on the one hand, we can be very ambitious, on the other, we also need to learn, appreciate, and acknowledge ways in which we can lead a fulfilling life by managing the changes caused due to uncertainty around us.

There are life skills that, if mastered, can help us throughout our lives. They are our companions and best friends in every situation and hence need to be practiced by everyone. The top quality we mention in this list is gratitude—our ability to be thankful for all that we have, allowing us to look at our situation differently with a certain bliss. This thought—'the situation is bad'—is significantly different from the feeling that 'the situation could have been worse'. We can all rue about what we didn't get, but at the same time, we can feel blessed about what we have.

One of the key secrets of living a happy life is practicing gratitude on a regular basis and in every situation. It not only builds our positive brain but also allows us to be ready for the surprises life throws at us. Through our stories from the cricketing field, we will demonstrate how leaders and players practicing gratitude scale stellar heights.

If we wish to cultivate a happier life, we should also be mindful of how authentic we are. Integrity is the quality that allows us to be truthful in every situation. This is what we want to demonstrate through a chapter dedicated to this topic, supported by stories from cricketing field. At the end of the day, integrity is practicing honesty and showing consistent adherence to one's morals and ethics.

However, one who practices integrity shouldn't judge someone else on the basis of their perspective and should try to put oneself in the shoes of the person who is being judged. This is called kindness, which is a virtue that holds people in good stead in whatever situation they find themselves. Kindness is an amazing trait to possess while navigating changes in life, yet it is quite underrated in today's world. But that is the reality, and we need to bring it to everyone's attention that practicing kindness in every situation allows us to be humane and tackle any issue with the right mindset. When you practice kindness, it rubs off on others, and they are willing to help you in whatever way they can. We have used several stories from cricket that demonstrate kindness and how it is practiced by different leaders so that you get an understanding of the practical aspects of being a kind person.

While kindness allows us to understand others and their emotions, it is not enough. We also need to cultivate adaptability, which comes from accepting who we are, what our situation is, and how it is aligned to the reality we want to build for ourselves. It's about accepting the reality and moving forward with a positive mindset. Often, situations in life do not meet our expectations, and in those situations, we have a choice: to brood and blame someone for it, or accept and make the best out of it. Leaders demonstrate this ability to bring out the best in them and their teams by adapting to situations and then making the most out of their resources. This mental framework is what differentiates them from an average person. Ultimately, those who lead fulfilling lives have a perspective in their life. It is about taking a step back from daily activities and thinking about the larger picture. Who are we? What are we doing? Why are we doing what we are doing? These are some important questions they reflect on and make sense of life. Without this perspective, the larger picture always remains a blur for the average person, and they continue to engage into day-to-day activities without grasping the larger picture. Without a unique perspective, we lead an ordinary life unbeknownst to the immense potential we possess.

This book is a journey where one first understands the nuances of becoming a better version of oneself by conquering the self and developing qualities essential to create self-awareness. It then moves towards managing relationships and building teams that work towards achieving unthinkable dreams in the face of a changing world. We hope you enjoy this journey.

SECTION I

MANAGING SELF

1

Hope

Clinging on to the Smallest of Support Systems and Making It Work for You

"HOPE IS THE COMPANION OF POWER, AND MOTHER OF SUCCESS; FOR WHO SO HOPES STRONGLY HAS WITHIN HIM THE GIFT OF MIRACLES."

—SAMUEL SMILES, British author

Hope—what a powerful and magical word! It is a word we become familiar with early on in our life, isn't it? Hope is something which has kept humankind alive despite the many adversities we have faced. It is like air—absolutely essential for our existence, and like breathing, it comes naturally to humans. Without hope, no life can prosper.

The world of cricket is full of unforgettable moments that allow us to witness the true character of people who are thrown into challenging situations. Every demanding situation makes cricketers think not only of themselves but also of their entire team. A small step in the right direction goes a long way in building positive mindset, which is an important ingredient for being a hopeful person.

The Indian Premier League (IPL)—the most popular cricket league in the world—has always been followed with great fervour by Indian and international cricket fans. We are all familiar with the so-called rivalry between the two strong teams: Mumbai Indians (MI) and Chennai Super Kings (CSK). With five wins each, it's a known fact that MI and CSK have been the most successful and best teams to play in the IPL. While CSK won their first by defeating MI in 2010, MI won their first title in 2013 and then saw a steady streak of wins in 2015, 2017, 2019, and 2020. MI was evidently struggling and had failed to bag a single trophy in the initial five seasons since the IPL began in 2008. They were a good team, but with no wins. So, what caused this turn around? What gave them hope?

In 2010, MI made it to the IPL finals for the first time, and were playing against MS Dhoni's CSK. This gave them the much-needed boost and bolstered their hope of winning the championship. At this stage, both the teams had not won a single title since 2008 and were practically sailing in the same boat. Although MI lost that final match against CSK, the impact and learning from that encounter served them well for future. Watching CSK play on the front foot in a high-octane match showed MI what can be achieved with sheer belief. Once the belief took root, MI did not look back. They just didn't give up and realized that although they have the mettle to win, their weakness lay in the execution. Behind the glimmer of trophies were the countless hours of meticulous practice sessions, sweat, hard work, and the precise execution of the roles given to everyone in the team, including the support staff. When all of this came together, the result was quite evident. Out of eight sessions since 2013, MI won the title five times. This is what hope can do. Once you start being positive, set your priorities, and know what you are capable of, it's all about putting your abilities to full use.

During the 2020 edition of the IPL tournament, Chennai Super Kings were derided as "Daddy's Army" by the critics because most of their players were over 30. In a high-intensity format like T20, it is considered a liability because the game demands agile and fittest athletes who don't lose energy for 40 overs. Mostly in CSK's playing 11, majority of the players were over 30 and some of the big players were no longer active in the international circuit. And the leaders of the ship were MS Dhoni (age 39) and another veteran from South Africa, Imran Tahir (age 41). Dhoni's team looked less like a modern IPL team, rather it reminded everyone of a veteran cricket team. Everyone started questioning the 'Dhoni model' of running a franchise. Questions were asked but Dhoni was unfazed. He didn't lose hope because he knew that one bad season doesn't define one's legacy. He stuck to his methods without uttering a word and in the very next year, 2021, came back to win the trophy for the fourth time.

There was no grand jubilation or wild celebration, just an acknowledgement that one task had been accomplished, and now it was time to move on to the next one. Being hopeful is the hallmark of those who believe in the process and they let the results speak for themselves. CSK's triumph

BEING HOPEFUL IS THE HALLMARK OF THOSE WHO BELIEVE IN THE PROCESS AND THEY LET THE RESULTS SPEAK FOR THEMSELVES

in 2021 was, once again, a vindication of the power of hope. It wasn't just Dhoni but the entire CSK team that remained hopeful of a magical turnaround because of their past deeds.

This is what hope looks like. When the chips are down and everyone thinks that you won't be able to rise again, you do, and prove everyone wrong. In your mind, there is no doubt about your success because you are positive and take every moment as it comes, without worrying about what has happened in the past or what the future holds. This is exactly what happened in the famous Kolkata Test match of 2001. On the fourth day, both Rahul Dravid and VVS Laxman were positive about the way they were playing without thinking too far ahead about the match or the result they hoped to achieve.

The Oxford dictionary defines 'hope' as a feeling of wanting something to happen and thinking that it is possible. Both Dravid and Laxman showed how to make something possible when it looks impossible through their positive mindset and optimistic outlook, despite the challenging situation they were in.

Hope Against Hope

Hope has such a profound effect on humans that we have the phrase "hope against hope." It essentially means that there are indeed some situations in life where there is no hope, no possibility of a miracle, yet we continue to hope, even though the outcome seems unlikely—like expecting a beautiful flower to bloom in the desert.

How many of you know the story behind Indian men's cricket team's first-ever Cricket World Cup win? It is one of the finest stories of hope triumphing over seemingly unsurmountable odds. The West Indies were the undisputed champions in the 1970s and 1980s. They were so dominant that that they hadn't lost a single match in the first two editions of World Cup. They won the 1975 and 1979 World Cup without facing a single defeat and were expected to win the third one in the same fashion. On the other hand, India hadn't won a single match against a top team in the World Cup. However, India's then captain, Kapil Dev, was a man full of hope. He believed in miracles and always hoped for new beginnings. He already had established himself as India's first world-class pace bowler, defying the popular belief that Indians could only excel in spin bowling.

June 25, 1983, inarguably, is a day which can be said as the one that changed not only Indian cricket but also the course of world cricket forever. If ever there was a glorious sporting triumph which truly captured the meaning of hope, this must surely count.

Even though India had won two memorable Test series in England and West Indies in 1971, beating the two-time champion West Indies in the 1983 Cricket World Cup seemed beyond imagination. Before anyone could simply dismiss India's win as a fluke, they must remember that in the very first match of the tournament, India halted the Caribbean team's unbeaten streak in World Cup matches. It was the West Indies' first loss in three World Cups. This gave India real hope when they met the same opponent on the most important day of their careers—the final. However, that hope was not the result of an overnight pep talk. Just before the World Cup, India had managed to pull off an unexpected win in the Caribbean. It was of immense importance, as it was only the second time the West Indies had lost a One Day International (ODI) game at home.

That victory perhaps played a crucial part in India's success, helping them win four matches in their group and make it to the semi-final for the first time. Throughout the campaign, India played as a determined unit, and the final was no different. There were no big innings—not even a half-century from a batsman—nor a five-wicket haul from the bowlers, and yet they won by 43 runs! Kris Srikkanth's 38 runs (the top score in the final) gave India early momentum, while Mohinder Amarnath (26 runs off 80 balls) and Sandeep Patil (27 runs off 29 balls) consolidated India in the middle. Later, Kapil Dev's 15, Madan Lal's 17, Syed Kirmani's 14, and Balwinder Sandhu's unbeaten 11 runs meant that everyone was hopeful of a win and hence every player did try their best, despite the odds being against them. A target of 184 runs in 60 overs seemed like a cakewalk for the competitive Caribbean team, but Sandhu's dismissal of the dangerous opener Gordon Greenidge on a single run was a sign that India's hope was well-founded. When Viv Richards, the mightiest of them all, hit 33 runs off just 28 balls with seven fours, Indian bowler Madan Lal cajoled his captain, Kapil Dev, to give him another over to ball, even though Viv Richards considered Madan Lal as non-threatening. It was only appropriate that Kapil Dev took the stunning catch which sent Richards back to the pavilion.

Among the top ten leading run scorers of the tournament, only Kapil Dev represented the champion side, while the runner-up West Indies had as many as four players on the list. The gulf between the two finalists could be understood from the above fact alone. A startling fact of the tournament was that, in the 40 ODIs before the World Cup, India had lost 28 matches. Not just that, in the previous two editions of the World Cup, India's only victory has been against a low-key associate nation like East Africa. However, that didn't bother the captain, who was an embodiment of hope. "I am very happy with what my team did today. We want to come here (to England) with the same spirit and win again. We played like winners in this match and throughout the tournament. Everybody fought, and they told me, 'We will do it,'" Kapil Dev had said after the historic win in his post-match presentation at Lord's balcony.

Hope is refusing to accept setbacks as the final result. Hope is acknowledging the universal fact that the sun will rise again, no matter how dark today seems. Hope gives us the reason to believe that any miracle is possible. Hope tells us that there is surprisingly no limit to human capacity to face challenges and conquer battles.

HOPE GIVES US THE REASON TO BELIEVE THAT ANY MIRACLE IS POSSIBLE

Another match etched in our memory is about a team that believed in winning in the face of great adversity. In the Antigua Test of 2003, the West Indies team were chasing 418 runs against a formidable Australian team. Until that time, no other team had chased as many runs to register a victory in Test cricket history. Not that chasing such a huge score was not possible, the general thinking was: if it hadn't been done before, it wasn't possible. There was no hope—or so it seemed. Brian Lara believed it was possible, as did Shivnarine Chanderpaul and Ramnaresh Sarwan. They all contributed with the bat and chased the impossible. While the world saw it as a hopeless situation, the West Indian batsmen believed it was possible. They were positive and played with an intent to win. They were not ready to give an extra inch to the opposition and put a price on their wicket.

This match is regarded as a classic David vs Goliath encounter in Test cricket. The Australians were at their domineering best at the time, while the West Indies, despite having a bunch of few exceptional players, were not considered a strong team. The visitors (Australia) had already won the first three matches of the series comprehensively and were looking for an unprecedented clean sweep in the Caribbean—a feat which no rival had ever achieved against the West Indies. However, the hosts hadn't lost hope, as their pride was at stake. They may have lost the series, but they didn't want an unprecedented humiliation of a 0-4 drubbing in their home soil.

What hope can do to someone, even in a seemingly hopeless situation, is exemplified by this miraculous victory of West Indies. Not only did they preserve their proud home record, but they also broke India's 27-year-old record for the highest run chase in a Test's final innings. Australia scored 240 in their first innings, and the West Indies responded with the same score in their response. At that moment, the West Indies began to believe they could match the Australians in St. John's stadium. The Australian openers, Matthew Hayden and Justin Langer, put up a partnership of 242 runs—just 2 more than the entire team managed in the first innings! The Aussies finished at 417 in their second innings, and undoubtedly, they were assured of a victory since they had one of the best bowling attacks. The West Indies began their chase as expected, losing their top 3 wickets for just 74 runs. Even if their captain, Brian Lara, tried to stem the tide, he fell at 165. However, Ramnaresh Sarwan and Shivnarine Chanderpaul didn't lose hope. Both scored centuries, but at 288 runs for 6 wickets, it seemed there could be only one winner: Australia. Chanderpaul, however, stayed at the crease, and somehow he managed to stretch the day and finished with West Indies at 371 for 6.

On the final day, the West Indies needed just 47 runs to secure a historic Test win. With Chanderpaul still at the crease, for the first time it appeared that the hosts were in control of an improbable chase. But then came the big blow by the Australians when their super pacer Brett Lee dismissed Chanderpaul at 104, leaving West Indies at 372 for 7 wickets. However, Sarwan and Chanderpaul had already revived the West Indian hope in such a great way that even the young and an inexperienced player like Omari Banks scored an unbeaten 47. He was complemented by Vasbert Drakes, who played a decisive cameo of 27. The two added unbeaten 46-run partnership for the eighth wicket, eventually turning the tables on the mighty Australians and making their 418-run chase the highest successful run chase in Test cricket history.

This is how hope triumphs against all odds. While you can't predict the future, you continue to encourage others with your positive intent. Hopeful people are inclusive and not exclusive; they have a vision and also the ability to manifest that vision. They know that if something needs to be done, it will be done, and if it requires others' help, they ensure it's achieved. This, again, reinforces the view that with their positive intent, they are able to align people in a positive way, and with collective force, no target is unachievable.

How to Build Hope

As human beings, we are bound to worry about how our future unfolds. When we think negatively about the future, worry creeps in. But when we remind ourselves of a positive outcome, hope germinates. We need to remember that worrying may not aide in improving our outcome, but being positive can. Such a frame of mind allows us to give our best and maintain a positive outlook, even in failure. Being hopeful helps us pick ourselves when we fall. It also prepares us well for unforeseen circumstances and allows us to learn from mistakes we make on our journey to becoming successful.

In July-August 2012, India's Rohit Sharma failed miserably in a five-match ODI series against Sri Lanka. He managed just 13 runs across five innings, looking hopeless. Critics kept talking about his privilege and how he was able to retain his place in the squad after such a poor series. However, his then captain, MS Dhoni, didn't lose hope in Sharma's ability. Dhoni calmly told him that his future won't be judged by just one series. Rohit Sharma played just one more match that year and failed again, scoring just 4 runs. Even his die-hard fans started losing hope but not Sharma. He knew it was just a phase and he kept practicing and enhancing his skills rather than dwelling on the criticism.

In just a year, Rohit Sharma made a spectacular turnaround. The year 2013 brought him new hope for a fresh start. And, what a turnaround it had been since then. Since 2013, Sharma became as successful as another popular Indian batsman Virat Kohli and went on to score five centuries in a single World Cup—a record no other player in the history had managed before. Furthermore, against the same opposition, Sri Lanka, in 2014, Rohit Sharma secured a world record of single-handedly scoring 264 runs in one innings—surpassing the score of the entire Sri Lankan team, which managed just 251 runs in that match! This is what hope does to an individual.

Rohit Sharma displayed another key trait of hopeful people:

regardless of the circumstances, favourable or unfavourable, they remain focused on the process. They continuously work on their skills because that's what is in their control. Their confidence stems from their efforts and the harder they work, the better becomes their chances to excel. That is what matters in the end.

Sharma is now a legend, but how many of you are aware of his struggle during his initial years as a cricketer? Hailed as one of the most gifted cricketers of his generation, Rohit Sharma had a fine start but struggled to translate his huge potential into something significant. It's like a student being seen as the most intelligent in the class, yet their report card doesn't reflect it.

In his first 98 ODI innings, Sharma had just scored two centuries and averaged 32.5—like a student who is expected to score over 90% in a subject managing only 60%. In his next 159 innings, he scored another 29 ODI centuries and averaged 49.16, close to 50, proving himself as a great player in one-day internationals. So, finally, he managed to score 90 plus! How was that possible? Purely because of hope. Never for a moment, Rohit Sharma doubted his ability, and importantly, his captain MS Dhoni, didn't lose hope either. A captain in a cricket team is like a parent: when your parents back you and never lose hope, the children generally do well.

Essential Character Traits of a Hopeful Person

1. **Being optimistic about the future:** Even when the chips are down, hopeful people believe that tough times won't last forever, and if they continue doing what they need to, success will follow.
2. **Accepting change:** Hopeful people are well aware of the fact that time doesn't stand still. They understand that not

all things are under their control. They accept and move forward without harbouring any negative thoughts. This is a key difference between hopeful people and others.

3. **Embracing failure:** For them, failure is not permanent. Each failure presents an opportunity to learn something new about themselves, their plans, and what else they can do to improve. Failure is not something to brood over; it's an opportunity to learn and prepare for the next attempt with confidence.

4. **Being inclusive, not exclusive:** Hopeful people, with their vision and positive approach, inspire others to join them and create a massive force in achieving any target they set. They recognize that everyone has the ability to contribute and express their talent to positively move towards their goals.

5. **Practice, practice, practice:** Confidence, positivity, and hope don't just happen. They are developed through consistent hard work. Be it summers or winters, they follow a routine and never shy away from hard work. Their consistent effort makes them confident of their chances, and this is why they appear hopeful to others.

2

Positivity

A Mindset that Makes You See the Glass Half Full

**"WHEN PEOPLE THROW STONES AT YOU,
YOU TURN THEM INTO MILESTONES."**

—SACHIN TENDULKAR, Indian cricket legend

How many professionals have received a raise of 5275%? It just sounds staggering, and indeed it is, because it is rarest of the rare occasions when something like this happens. However, when this happens to someone who was never perceived as particularly gifted or a prodigy, people may term it a lucky break. Only five cricketers have seen their previous IPL salary rise by 2000% and more. And when right-arm bowler Harshal Patel was brought back by Royal Challengers Bangalore for ₹10.75 crore (USD 1.4 million) during the mega auction in early February 2022, it reaffirmed what positivity can do to someone's life.

"Whether you're playing or not, contribute in a positive manner. Smile; don't spread negativity. I have seen many times when you're not playing, it's easy to get bitter. It's easy to think,

'I'm better than the guy playing,' but when you start thinking like that, you add negative energy to the environment, and nobody likes that. So, wait for your turn, help in whatever way you can, put the team first, do everything for the greater cause—which is to contribute to the success of the team. If you do that, people will realize: this guy is a positive influence. When you don't do well, these are the things that go in your favour," explained Harshal Patel in an interview with *ESPNcricinfo.com* on the importance of maintaining a consistent positive mindset.

Harshal Patel is someone who has seen it all—both highs and lows—on the cricket field. He had a dream start when he represented India in the 2010 Under-19 World Cup in New Zealand and soon bagged an IPL contract with the Mumbai Indians. However, things were not always rosy; in fact, he couldn't even make it to his state's (Gujarat) first-class team. Yet, he never allowed negativity to cloud his thoughts. He moved to the state of Haryana to pursue his dream and made his IPL debut for Royal Challengers Bangalore (RCB) against Delhi Daredevils (DD) in the 2012 edition. However, from 2012 to 2014, he didn't have a single standout IPL performance. While his first-class form suffered in between, he made a strong comeback in the 2015-16 cricket season. His tally of 22 wickets in Ranji Trophy 2015-16 added to a haul of 13 wickets in the Vijay Hazare Trophy, in which he also picked up his maiden List A five-for.[1]

From 2016 to 2020, Patel just played on and off but he kept learning new skills, and his belief in positivity remained

---

[1] ESPN Digital Media Private Limited. 2024. "Harshal Patel Profile - Cricket Player India | Stats, Records, Video." ESPNcricinfo. May 5, 2024. https://www.espncricinfo.com/cricketers/harshal-patel-390481.

unshaken. So much so that when he was picked by DD for a modest salary of ₹20 lakh for the season, he didn't feel dejected. Even when DD did not retain him in 2021 and he was traded back to his old team (RCB), Patel finally found his footing. He became the most successful bowler in the IPL, with a record haul of 32 wickets that season. Everything started falling into place, from an astounding salary hike to wearing the India cap. Needless to say, it wasn't possible without a positive attitude—not just towards his game but towards life as well.

In life, you'll face many situations that don't go your way. It can be difficult for people to remain positive in such circumstances, but those who can stay positive even in adversity gain a lot when it comes to both mental and physical benefits. A positive mindset positively impacts physical health which is the most crucial aspect for sportsmen. For instance, a research—conducted by Johns Hopkins expert Lisa R. Yanek, M.P.H., and her colleagues[2]—shows that people with a positive outlook and a family history of heart diseases are one-third less likely to suffer from a heart attack or other cardiovascular event between 5 to 25 years of their life, compared to those with a more negative outlook. The study further held that positive individuals, even with family histories who had the highest risk factors for coronary artery disease, were 13 percent less likely than their negative counterparts to have a heart attack or other coronary event.

Positivity is defined as the state of being or tendency to be positive or optimistic, whatever the situation may be. Many

---

[2] (Yanek et al. 2013) "Effect of Positive Well-Being on Incidence of Symptomatic Coronary Artery Disease." The American Journal of Cardiology 112 (8): 1120–25. https://doi.org/10.1016/j.amjcard.2013.05.055.

assume that positive thinking means being happy all the time or never dealing with negativity; this is a wrong assumption. Truth be told, everyone experiences negativity in their life. A person with a positive mindset faces negative moments in constructive way. While many of us may lose our composure in the face of negativity around us, there are a few with the right approach who convert it into a positive mindset. It all depends upon how our mind speaks to us—our self-talk. To change the way we think, we need to look closely into how we think in the first place. We need to dig deeper and find from where these self-talks take root.

Self-Talk

Positive thinking, like negative, often starts with self-talk. Most of the time, we are constantly talking to ourselves. It is like having a constant internal monologue running through your head, which is not spoken but heard by your mind. These thoughts can either be positive or negative; some can arise from your logic or reason and, at times, it can be illogical and baseless. Sometimes it arises from misconceptions that you create because of lack of information. Often, these thoughts can also arise from certain preconceived assumptions we have about things, events, or people around us. For instance, sometimes we think: "Oh, this person didn't greet me despite seeing me, is it something to do with my appearance or is he simply in a hurry?" There are several such instances, but all of these cross our minds based on what assumptions we make. Depending on what we assume, our self-talk can be either positive or negative. The problem is, many of us are unaware of whether our thoughts are positive or negative or even where exactly they come from.

With little awareness and understanding, we can not only recognize our thoughts but also learn how to deal with them. Here are a few reasons why negative thoughts germinate:

1. **Filtering:** In this situation, your mind solely focuses on the negative aspects of a situation, leaving behind the positives. For example, you delivered an amazing lecture in your college, and everyone complimented you except for one person. Your mind can ask you to ignore all the positive comments that were made on the report and make you dwell on the negative ones which, in turn, lead you into a negative self-talk mindset.

2. **Personalizing:** Here you take all the blame if any situation goes south. If something bad happens or a task is not accomplished, your mind convinces you that you are responsible for it. If only you were better or perfect, the situation could have been different. For instance, all your friends go to a movie and didn't ask you to join in, you'd assume that you are not good enough to be a part of that group and it's your fault that you are not invited to group outings. This line of thinking gives rise to negativity and negative self-talk.

3. **Catastrophizing**: In this situation, you automatically anticipate the worst possible outcome in any circumstance you are in. Suppose you are playing a game of chess with your friend and you make a mistake. This mistake makes

you extremely stressed because you believe that it's going to cost you the match and you wish if only you could go in the past and correct things. Since you can't do it, you believe that there is no way out from the situation you are in and losing the match, series, and reputation is inevitable.

These three aspects are the main reasons for negative self-talk. So, before trying to understand how negative emotions or events can be converted into positive, we need to first understand the basic reason why these thoughts arise and how we should address them.

Let's look at another example from cricket: Indian right-handed batter Shreyas Iyer went through the phases of negative self-talk but never allowed these thoughts to take permanent hold. As a result, he could make a terrific comeback each time when things seemed tougher.

Shreyas Iyer came into limelight for the first time during the 2014 Under-19 World Cup. He made his first-class debut in the Ranji Trophy for Mumbai soon after, and by 2017, he was playing for India in both ODI and T20 formats. Things were going well for him when he was chosen as captain of the IPL team from Delhi mid-way through the 2018 season, replacing the successful Gautam Gambhir and led the Delhi Capitals (DC) squad to their first IPL playoffs in 2019. Play-off means securing a spot among top four teams which Delhi Capitals hadn't done for the last seven seasons.

The following year, in 2020, DC team made it to the IPL final. However, things took a turn when Iyer was ruled out for the first half of the 2021 season due to a shoulder injury during the ODI series at home against England. While he was recovering from his shoulder surgery, Rishabh Pant was named interim captain for the first half of the 2021 season and was retained for the position even when Iyer returned for the second half of IPL 2021 season in the UAE. Once the season got over, Shreyas Iyer was not among the four players (Rishabh Pant, Axar Patel, Prithvi Shaw, and Anrich Nortje) to be retained by DC ahead of the mega auction in 2022.

These setbacks did shake Iyer's confidence, however, he was not the one to blame others for his misfortune. In fact, his positive outlook made him one of the costliest buys in the IPL auction 2022 as he was roped in by Kolkata Knight Riders (KKR) for ₹12.25 crore and the icing on the cake was that now he was appointed as the captain again. This same positive approach towards life and his game earned him a Man of the Series award against Sri Lanka in February 2022 when some of the top guns like Virat Kohli were given a break.

Now, suddenly, Iyer's international career was back on track and everything else was falling in place for him. He, in fact, made it to the Test team as well, the ultimate dream for any cricketer. The power of positivity transformed him. "I was in a good frame of mind and then that injury began playing on my mind. Forced breaks are never easy because you have to start all over again. Injuries and rehabs are painful. But I must say, it turned out to be a blessing in disguise. The injury had made me feel I was 50% of the player I otherwise am. Having fully recovered, I've come back fresh and feel good. So, whatever happens, happens for good," revealed Iyer in an interview with *The Times of India*[3].

---

[3] Rao, K Shriniwas. 2022. "Whatever We Are Doing on the Field Right Now Is Preparation for the T20 World Cup, Says Shreyas Iyer." The Times of India, March 1, 2022. https://timesofindia.indiatimes.com/sports/cricket/sri-lanka-in-india/int20s-%20its-a-crime-if-you-play-a-dot-ball-shreyas-iyer/articleshow/89912453.cms.

Almost all negative emotions stem from blaming others for negative situations that occur. The problem arises when people hold on to these emotions, even when they can't change the outcome and feel angry about it.

The key to eliminating negative emotion is to take responsibility for yourself, your reactions, and your circumstances. As we just saw in case of Iyer, he never blamed anyone for his setbacks. It's crucial to remind yourself that some things are not under your control, while there are many which are within your circle of influence. Positive people perceive challenges as an opportunity to test themselves, build character, and learn lessons.

> **THE KEY TO ELIMINATING NEGATIVE EMOTIONS IS TO TAKE RESPONSIBILITY FOR YOURSELF, YOUR REACTIONS, AND YOUR CIRCUMSTANCES**

Another trait of positive individuals is that they are aware that no one in the world can make them feel negative without their permission. They know that they can choose how to respond in any situation. Instead of reacting impulsively, they keep their calm and trust their instincts in the face of adversity.

Sometimes people embrace failures because they realize that it offers an opportunity to learn something new. So, in case they fail, they take it with positive intent and a vow to bounce back stronger. Sporting history is filled with countless stories around the same where seemingly hopeless situations were turned around by those who had been in situations like this in the past.

In the last 70 years or so, India had managed to win just one Test series in Australia, in 2019, when Virat Kohli was captain. As the most successful captain and one of the all-time great batsmen, Kohli was being hailed as the single most important factor for this historic win. However, when India toured Australia for an encore in 2020 (The Border-Gavaskar Trophy), they were brutally jolted by the hosts in Adelaide, where they were infamously bundled out for a mere 36 runs. After the humiliation, Kohli returned to India on paternity leave, and in such unusual circumstances, Ajinkya Rahane took over the captaincy for the next match (the Melbourne Test) and the rest of the series. Soon, the new captain was walking in to bat at 64 for 3 in response to Australia's 195. This was the turning point of the match, as Rahane's cheap dismissal could have easily made the Australia's comeback easier. Rahane's incredible century (112) that rescued India's tour could be counted as one of the best examples of rising to the occasion. Not only did Rahane bat with a remarkable positivity, he also radiated that same belief among his teammates.

The first thing he did as captain was to tell everyone that the Adelaide disaster was a closed chapter. "I told them that the topic should not be discussed at all," Rahane told *Sakal*, a leading Marathi daily[4]. "The fact that we were all out for 36 is not any mistake. We should just accept it and move on. No point in analyzing it deeply because the [next Test] match was starting in three days. My only message was: it happened in

---

[4] ESPNcricinfo. 2021. "How Ajinkya Rahane and His Trusted Lieutenants Masterminded India's Border-Gavaskar Triumph." ESPNcricinfo, January 24, 2021. https://www.espncricinfo.com/story/aus-vs-ind-2020-21-howajinkya-%20rahane-and-his-trusted-lieutenants-masterminded-india-striumph-%201249070

one hour. They [Australia] played good cricket. Such things happen once in a century. The faster we accept it and move on, the better for us."

Rahane and his team had some daunting odds to overcome in such a short span of time. Three first-choice players were missing, the team was still reeling from being all out for 36 and to make matters worse, Rahane lost a crucial toss in his first match as captain in that series. Yet, with positive intent, he orchestrated one of their greatest comebacks in India's Test cricket history away from home.

"The captain's century came at a time when India could easily have faded to a two-nil deficit, and it was this performance that gave his team the conviction that victory was attainable," wrote former Australia captain Ian Chappell in glowing praise of the Indian batsman. More than a superstar like Kohli or Dhoni, it is easier to identify oneself with a seemingly average person like Rahane. He isn't a superstar, and his struggles and failures often are forgotten because he has consistently made comebacks.

Another aspect of what makes people positive is the fact that they concentrate more on the process than worrying about outcomes. It's important to create a roadmap for yourself after assessing where you are and where you want to go, and then stick to your plan with utmost discipline. In such situations, success is not an accident but the result of relentless pursuit of excellence through discipline, dedication, and determination. In scenarios like this, you are bound to be positive.

People are also known to emulate the characteristics of the company they keep. When you are surrounded by positive people, your positivity increases because there are people who cheer you up despite the situation you are in. Good leaders always build their team consciously and surround themselves with positive people. Not only do they engage in positive self-talk, but they also encourage others when they are down. Affirmations by individuals and teams goes a long way in building the future they visualize.

GOOD LEADERS ALWAYS BUILD THEIR TEAM CONSCIOUSLY AND SURROUND THEMSELVES WITH POSITIVE PEOPLE

Sometimes, people wonder how one can remain positive in challenging circumstances. Can this be learned? Because there are very few people around us who are positive despite any obstacles they face, and then there are others who are perennially pessimistic.

Learning to be positive may sound tough, but here is some good news: you can learn to turn your negative thinking into positive. It is not that difficult a process but it requires a lot of effort, time, and practice. It is like building a new habit, and habits take effort and patience to form. Here are some practical ways to think and behave more positively and optimistically:

1. **Identify areas to change:** Changing everything in one go is not possible, nor is it a good strategy. The first step towards being optimistic and practicing positive thoughts is to identify the areas of your life that are generally negative. Whether it's your work, your marriage, your commute, or anything which has a lot of negativity attached to it. You can start with one area, and try to find something positive within the heap of negativity which surrounds it. Slowly but surely, you will start realizing that it's not as bad as it initially looked, and from there, your road to positivity will begin.

2. **Check yourself:** We generally think a lot during the day without even realizing what we are thinking. It is always a good idea to take a pause and reflect on our thoughts. If you catch yourself thinking negatively at any given time, you need to make a note and find a way to focus on something positive at that moment. Maybe it's a bad start for the day at work, but a congratulatory email from a client was a good thing. Or, the traffic is quite bad, but the ability to listen to a good audiobook during this time makes up for it. You may surprise yourself with the ubiquity of positivity around you if you choose to notice it.

3. **Be open to humour:** We tend to take life too seriously, and often for good reason. We have deadlines, pressure to complete tasks, or a goal to pursue, and in all this, we forget to laugh. An important thing to note is that life is not as serious as we think it is. During the day, we need to find moments or events that make us laugh and bring our lighter side to the fore. We need to give ourselves the permission to be light-hearted and smile as frequently as we can. In fact, if we can smile during tough times, we will certainly face these challenges in a better way. After a string of failures in IPL 2022, you could still see Virat Kohli undeterred and letting out a smile. Tough times will come and go, but your attitude towards life and your ability to smile in the face of challenges will take you far.

4. **Follow a healthy lifestyle:** A positive mind resides in a healthy body. Do take care of your body; prioritize your health. Ensure that exercise becomes an integral part of your daily routine—if not much, then you can dedicate at least 30 minutes in a day to it. You will be able to see the positive impact it has on your mood and how it helps

reduce stress. Having a healthy diet and enough sleep are also crucial for keeping your mind fresh, and a fresh mind naturally encourages positive thoughts.

5. **Practice positive self-talk:** In our daily lives, there are several instances where we feel bad about ourselves and the situations we are in. If we follow a simple rule of reminding ourselves that we will not engage in negative self-talk no matter the situation we are in, it will keep us in good stead. Remind yourself of not saying anything that you wouldn't say to someone else then it is a great start. We need to teach ourselves to be gentle, kind, and encouraging with ourselves first. This will be a good way to protect ourselves from letting a negative thought enter our minds. However, if a negative thought does arise, evaluate it rationally and respond with affirmations and reminders of what is good about you. Think about things you're thankful for in your life.

Positivity plays a crucial role in our lives, helping us prepare to face any situation. Staying positive is an essential trait to lead a balanced and happy life. With a positive mindset, even the worst circumstances can be handled with ease, which is one of the reasons why successful people become so successful.

3

Resilience

Rise like a Phoenix from the Ashes

**"IT ALWAYS SEEMS IMPOSSIBLE
UNTIL IT'S DONE."**

—NELSON MANDELA, South African anti-apartheid activist,
politician, and statesman

Today, almost every other child playing cricket in India aspires to be the next Virat Kohli. Kohli, unquestionably, is the most influential cricketer of modern times. He's revered not only in India but also across the world, and has gained similar adulation as the iconic cricket veterans—Sir Vivian Richards and Sachin Tendulkar. It is, of course, always easy to remember and be fascinated by Kohli's success and popularity since he is a hugely accomplished cricketer. Off the field, too, he leads a glamorous life with millions of followers on social media and numerous domestic and global brand endorsements to his name. However, even someone as exceptional and talented as Kohli encounters failures; no one thinks of that. Like any other human being, Kohli, too, faced several disappointing moments in his career. He was dropped right after his first Test series in

West Indies in 2011 as he had failed to grab the opportunities with both hands. He had scored only 76 runs in the three-match series at an average of 15.20 and was dismissed by West Indies bowler Fidel Edwards three times out of five innings.[1] However, he made a comeback soon after with twin fifties and is now regarded as one of the best cricketers to have played the highest format of the game.

Virat Kohli epitomizes the virtues of resilience. In his first England tour in 2014, Kohli performed miserably. With scores of 1, 8, 25, 0, 39, 28, 0,7, 6, and 20 in the five Tests, Kohli averaged just 13.50 across 10 innings. However, in his next tour of England, he scored a record 593 runs. In 5 Tests, Kohli scored nearly 600 runs at an average of 59.30 and finished the series as the highest run-getter. In 2014, he managed just 134 runs in 5 Tests, but also scored more than 149 runs in just one innings. This upturn was due to his resilient nature. "A lot of people consider good tours as a milestone, but for me that tour of 2014 is always going to be the milestone in my career from where I thought things might go bad for me very soon," Kohli had said in an interview with Mayank Agarwal for the *BCCI. tv's* Open Nets. Kohli's ability to bounce back from hopeless situations and win is what makes him a true champion.

What Is Resilience?

The Oxford Dictionary defines resilience as the ability of people or things to recover quickly from something unpleasant, such as

---

[1] Nair, Gokul. "'My First Series Was a Disappointment' - When Virat Kohli Addressed a Press Conference after His First Ever Test Fifty in 2011." Sportskeeda, September 16, 2024. https://www.sportskeeda.com/cricket/my-first-series-disappointment-when-virat-kohli-addressed-press-conference-first-ever-test-fifty-2011.

a shock or an injury. Needless to say that it's one of the most important character traits of a successful person, regardless of the field they are in. No matter who we are or how successful we may have been, we will experience failures and setbacks. If we haven't yet (let's thank our lucky stars!), then most likely we would at some point. If your mindset is that of a champion, you will always strive to be better and challenge yourself. With such a mindset, setbacks are inevitable. Thus, it is crucial to face these challenges thinking that you are having just another bad day and move on. Any sport, after all, teaches us that there is always another match to make a comeback, another series to perform, and another trophy to win. No matter the challenges, we must make a comeback—stronger, fitter, and better.

NO MATTER WHO WE ARE OR HOW SUCCESSFUL WE MAY HAVE BEEN, WE WILL EXPERIENCE FAILURES AND SETBACKS

Why Resilience Is So Important?

Resilience is crucial because we face failures more often than we taste success. Even the most iconic sportsmen, like Sachin Tendulkar, have faced struggles in their coveted careers, forget the lesser mortals. So, unless you are not resilient, you will quit at the first sign of misery or hardship. As human beings, resilience comes naturally to us. From crawling, stumbling, and learning to walk, we instinctively pick ourselves up and try again. As kids, when we learn to ride a bicycle, we wobble and fall several times, and yet we never refuse to learn.

Subconsciously, we understand that falling is inevitable and we can only learn to ride if we stand back on our feet again. Eventually, bicycle riding becomes second nature.

Even though cricket and many other sports are primarily team games, an exceptionally resilient character (team member) can transform the fortune of the entire team. Do you remember the 2016 ICC World Twenty20—the sixth edition of the ICC Men's T20 World Cup final between England and the West Indies in Kolkata? The West Indies needed 19 runs in the last over to win. The pressure was immense, especially on the West Indies. While the Caribbean team was studded with star cricketers like Chris Gayle, Andre Russell, and Dwayne Bravo who were already established champions in the T20 format, England, on the other hand, had never won a global trophy until then. The West Indies waltzed through the tough over with their all-rounder Carlos Brathwaite smashing four consecutive sixes off a young and talented Ben Stokes leading his team to a jaw-dropping victory! It was indeed an astonishing sight for cricket fans but a tragic moment for Stokes who let the World T20 final slip from England's grasp.

"Ben Stokes sees his world collapse after Carlos Brathwaite's T20 blast," wrote *The Guardian*. Stokes was crestfallen. Till then, only two international cricketers—former South African opening batter H.H. Gibbs and former Indian all-rounder Yuvraj Singh—had humiliated their bowlers in a similar fashion in the history of World Cups by hitting six consecutive sixes in a single over. The guilt of losing a World Cup final can overwhelm anyone but Stokes chose resilience. He didn't let this personal setback and team's defeat define him. Just as in life, you get a chance to redeem yourself in sports as well. This happens only if you believe that when the time arrives, you will grab the opportunity with both hands and never allow the nightmare of the past to cloud your thinking and judgment.

Fast forward to the 2019 ICC Cricket World Cup final (50 overs); it is England vs New Zealand. This time, instead of bowling, Stokes was batting. Stokes redeemed himself by playing an innings of 84 to tie the match in an unbelievable fashion and played a major role in leading England to victory. The same newspaper, *The Guardian,* ran the headline—Ben Stokes writes his redemption story with World Cup tour de force.

Indeed, Stokes' story is powerful, dramatic, and awe-inspiring in equal measure. More than anything else, it speaks about the human capacity to redeem oneself. Interestingly, the resilience shown by Stokes was not just restricted to the cricket pitch. He has seen a few hiccups in personal life as well. Almost a year before this 2019 World Cup final, Stokes was publicly humiliated for his poor performance on field.

Furthermore, in the wee hours of September 25, 2017, Stokes was arrested for his involvement in a brawl outside a pub in Bristol (England) and subsequently released under investigation. He was out with his teammate Alex Hales celebrating the team's win over West Indies in the third ODI played on September 24. The news of his arrest stunned the cricketing world and Stokes had to face a lot of criticism and public backlash. There were short- and long-term consequences of his arrest. For one, both Stokes and Hales were pulled out of the 4th ODI match against West Indies; Stokes was still injured by the time the fifth match was played. He was then removed from the squad due to impending outcome of the legal proceedings for the prestigious The Ashes Test series, which was to be played in Australia. If that wasn't enough, in the aftermath of the incident, Stokes lost a personal sponsorship contract and the vice-captaincy of the England cricket team. All this could have broken a weak-minded person, but not Stokes, who seemingly has a unique resilient bone in his body.

So, what makes Stokes thrive in such high-pressure situations? Mental toughness and resilience—the belief that consistently reminds you that you can always make a comeback. Stokes was born in New Zealand and his parents shifted to England when he was a child. His family had suffered a tragic loss (*The Sun* tabloid gracelessly revealed his personal story after the World Cup win and was criticized by everyone for its poor timing and taste), yet the young Stokes never allowed that unfortunate incident to ruin his future. Life is not fair, and we all have our own problems to deal with. This is a fact of life. Yet, those who have the will to fight, no matter the circumstances, are real winners. If you are not resilient, you won't survive. Even the greatest and mightiest face failures, but if you can make more comebacks than surrenders, you are often going to be a champion—just like Stokes.

How to Build Resilience

By trusting your ability. By refusing to accept setbacks as permanent. Ironical as it may sound, the best way to build resilience is to encounter enough failures in your career and life. Unless you fail, unless you get hurt, how will you know how to respond to such situations? And

UNLESS YOU FAIL, UNLESS YOU GET HURT, HOW WILL YOU KNOW HOW TO RESPOND TO SUCH SITUATIONS?

once you make a comeback, it reinforces your self-belief. It tells you: "If I can fight back and win once, I can do it again." That's how all sportspersons think instinctively.

FAILURES AND UNFULFILLED GOALS ARE A PART AND PARCEL OF A SPORTSPERSON'S LIFE

Failures and unfulfilled goals are a part and parcel of a sportsperson's life. Getting up and preparing for the fight despite the setback is something all sportspersons are aware of, especially those primed for greatness. So, what makes them so resilient?

Let us give you another example of a player from English cricket: Stuart Broad. Broad is one of the most successful bowlers in the history of Test cricket who retired with 604 wickets to his name (and overall 847 International wickets if one adds his white-ball cricket numbers). In 2020, while England was playing against West Indies, he wasn't chosen for the first match and was furious about his exclusion. He even vented his frustration in a TV interview on *Sky Sports*. "I'm not a particularly emotional person, but I've found the last couple of days quite tough," Broad said. "To say I'm disappointed would be an understatement—you get disappointed if you drop your phone and the screen breaks. I've been frustrated, angry, and gutted because it's quite a hard decision to understand."

A mature cricket board and team management took his comments sportingly, and Broad, for his part, made a stunning comeback and walked the talk. He single-handedly won back-to-back Test matches, helping his team win the series 2-1 despite trailing 0-1 after the first match. This was partly possible because of his resilience. Almost 13 years earlier, as a young prodigy, Broad was humiliated by India's Yuvraj Singh in a T20 World Cup match, where he was ingloriously and infamously hit for six consecutive sixes. This could have easily broken a young kid at the beginning of his career. However, Broad wasn't the one to give up easily. Having grown up in a cricketing family, he had witnessed his father's failures in his career. He took the ignominy in the right spirit and decided to improve himself. When a definitive account of his career will be written, there may be a mention of being hit for six 6s in an over, but mostly it will be about the glory he brought to himself and his team. And what's more, even his so-called nemesis applauded him for his resilience.

"I'm sure every time I write something about @StuartBroad8, people relate it to him getting hit for 6 sixes! Today, I request all my fans to applaud what he has achieved! 500 Test wickets is no joke—it takes hard work, dedication, and determination. Broady, you're a legend! Hats off," wrote Yuvraj Singh on his X (formerly Twitter) feed in complete admiration.

What Happens to Those Who Are Not Resilient?

Anyone who has heard childhood stories of the legendary cricketer Sachin Tendulkar is probably also aware of the story of his childhood friend and former dashing left-hander batsman Vinod Kambli. Many still believe he was as precocious as Tendulkar and they put on a world-record of unbroken 664-run partnership in a school match for fun. Kambli started his Test career in a stunning fashion, hitting two double-centuries and two hundreds in his first seven Tests. Kambli's Test average 54.20 is still better than the career averages of Rahul Dravid,

Virender Sehwag, and VVS Laxman. Yet, he played only 17 Tests for India. His last Test was in 1995, before he had even turned 24. Kambli's story is often recalled with a question: 'What went wrong?' The simple answer is that the left-hander wasn't resilient enough to make a comeback after facing his first major obstacle. In 1995, during a tour of India, the West Indian pacers exposed his vulnerability towards their hostile fast bowling, particularly short-pitched balls, and Kambli was never able to recover from that. This led to his downfall in this highest format of the game.

Another cricketer whose career fizzled out after early success was Laxman Sivaramakrishnan. Sivaramakrishnan made his Test debut as a 17-year-old against the West Indies and played a pivotal role in India's triumph at the World Championship of Cricket in 1985 in Australia. He had stunned the cricketing world by claiming three successive six-wicket-hauls in Test cricket. That was it. Despite this promising start, his career was soon over and he didn't even manage ten Tests for India.

Similarly, Shaun Tait (Australia), Brett Lee (Australia), and Shoaib Akhtar (Pakistan) were fast bowlers of this century who could bowl the quickest; at 100 mph, they could intimidate batsmen and break several bones. Fast bowling needs tremendous muscle strength and speed and all these three bowlers faced career-threatening injuries and challenges. Undeterred by these difficulties, Lee went on to become one of the greats, and Akhtar, despite the controversies in his career, made his mark and played 46 Tests. Tait, on the other hand, could play only three. Former Australian pacer Geoff Lawson summed it beautifully in *The Cricket Monthly*[2]: "He [Tait]

---

[2] 2015, January. "The Biggest Unfulfilled Talent." Cricinfo, January 1, 2015. https://www.thecricketmonthly.com/story/816423/-the-biggest-unfulfilled-talent.

always looked like an injury waiting to happen, and that was how his career was to unfold, with knee, shoulder, elbow, and back issues." Tait failed to exhibit the same resilience that made his contemporaries Lee and Akhtar successful despite facing the same challenges.

To put it briefly, resilience is the ability to rise after falling down. Everyone experiences setbacks, but it's only the resilient person who remains undeterred and tries harder the next time.

4

Discipline

Try Again and Again and Again, Without Complaints

"DISCIPLINE IS THE BRIDGE BETWEEN GOALS AND ACHIEVEMENTS."

—JIM ROHN, American entrepreneur, author, and motivational speaker

What Is Discipline?

What comes into our mind when we think of the word 'discipline'? Most of us immediately associate the word 'discipline' with some sort of punishment or restraint. Merriam-Webster's dictionary defines it as: 'control gained to punish or penalize for the sake of enforcing obedience and perfecting moral character.' However, this doesn't completely justify the essence of the word; we'd rather prefer another definition we came across online: *Discipline is when one uses reason to determine the best course of action regardless of one's desires.* That itch to watch a movie a little longer than planned, the temptation to eat that junk food while promising it's the last time—these and many such similar moments in life define how much discipline we live with.

If you want to lead an efficient and effective life, discipline provides you with the rules to do so. With discipline, you can make sacrifices which may not seem important in the short term but make a significant difference in the

> **IF YOU WANT TO LEAD AN EFFICIENT AND EFFECTIVE LIFE, DISCIPLINE PROVIDES YOU WITH THE RULES TO DO SO**

long term. Take, for instance, the fitness regime of former India captain Virat Kohli. Through immense discipline, he was able to change the perception of fitness not only in the realm of Indian cricket but also in world cricket.

Perhaps, we are all familiar with stories about Kohli being a foodie and taking his fitness lightly during the initial years of his career. He always knew that he was blessed with exceptional talent as a cricketer, as did the world. However, one day he realized that if he didn't work on his fitness in a very disciplined manner, he would not be able to achieve his full potential. Since then, his devotion to his fitness has become legendary. "My game will be nothing if I am not intense enough on the field and that is one of the main reasons why I keep working hard on my fitness. But now, it has become more of a second nature and my lifestyle. I would rather miss a practice session but not my training session. That's how important it has become for me," Kohli revealed in an interview with the *Hindustan Times* in November 2017.

We all are aware of Kohli's calibre as a batsman, but not many know this side of him being a strict disciplinarian when it comes to health and fitness. This explains that leading a disciplined life can profoundly affect one's career.

Discipline creates habits, habits form routines, and routines turn you into who you are. This focus on making your each day better eventually helps you lead a better life

overall. The great mental performance coach Brian Cain states, *"Today + Today + Today = Your Life"*. For most people, it is not about the talent you are born with or the opportunities you get, it is about the amount of discipline you display in your chosen field and your ability to resist temptations.

It's a common belief that some people are born with innate self-discipline and can effortlessly practice self-control (maybe like former India captain Rahul Dravid who is known for his solid discipline and unwavering focus). But the reality is that discipline, like a muscle, can be built over time. Like physical strength, discipline also becomes stronger if you work on it with conscious effort.

Time and again, sports stories show that disciplined teams end up skillfully outplaying the undisciplined ones. In recent times, no other team exhibits this quality better than New Zealand's cricket team. The Kiwis made it to the consecutive ICC ODI World Cup finals (in 2015 and 2019) and lost the 2019 edition due to an unfortunate and bizarre rule. Yet, they didn't lose heart and won the first-ever World Test Championship in June 2021 by beating a much talented and superior Indian side. They also made it to the final of the

T20 World Cup in UAE in October 2021. It's an incredible achievement for a country of just five million to reach the finals in all three contrasting formats of cricket (Test, ODI, and T20). New Zealand doesn't boast as many gifted cricketers at its disposal as India, Pakistan, or Australia, and yet they are one of the dominant forces in cricket. Much of the credit for their success goes to the disciplined nature of Kiwi cricketers who are taught from the beginning that discipline and hard work are the surest paths to glory.

Disciplined teams are able to see the big picture and exercise restraint during adversity. Teams that lack discipline lose their cool and often end up costing themselves a shot. Discipline is not built overnight; it is cultivated over days, months, and years of doing something consistently and not wavering from the path that defines their success. It involves holding each other accountable and supporting those who might have less self-control when it comes to doing things that others aren't willing to do.

People who have a great deal of discipline are able to overcome short-term temptations for long-term benefits. They are aware of how their actions today will shape the destiny they are trying to build for themselves. Zig Ziglar, the famous author and salesman, once told a story about traveling late at night, and getting into bed at 4 a.m., and then waking up just an hour and a half later to an alarm at 5:30 a.m. It would have been extremely difficult for a person, who has barely slept, to wake up at the sound of alarm. But it was not the case with Ziglar; he woke up because of the commitment he had made and there was no way he could not have wavered from it.

Ziglar, admittedly, had a horrible day and wasn't productive at all. Yet, he said that that decision changed his life. According to him, the simple act of getting up and resisting the temptation to switch off his alarm and stay in bed ensured that he sent a signal to his brain that it's not okay to make an exception. Had he given in that morning, a week later, he might have made another exception with the rational that he got only a few hours of sleep the previous night. Gradually, his brain would tell him that it's okay to make exceptions from the set routine.

Such exceptions eventually turn into habits of breaking discipline, a set structure and way of doing things. Those who want to cultivate a disciplined life have to be mindful about these exceptions; they may seem comforting for the time being, but they tend to alter your thought process by telling you 'it's okay' every time you choose them over your set routine. This little deviation in that crucial decisive moment leads to several more moments of deviations, ultimately ruining the structure you have built for yourself in your journey towards greatness. Great people are different and put a conscious effort to ensure that they do not succumb to such temptations and are extremely cautious about how they deal with the exceptions in life. Winning those micro moments helps them win the macro battles and they know it well.

Self-discipline is challenging because it requires you to work against your natural tendencies to do what is normal, comfortable, and at times, easy to adopt. In a way, it's like you're fighting with yourself. One part of your mind encourages you to eat that bag of chips, whereas the other dissuades you from consuming junk food. Sometimes, a part of you wants to smoke, but another part reminds you that it's harmful to your lungs. Now, which side wins? It all depends on what we tell our minds and how we exercise our willpower. If we tell ourselves, "It's okay to have one bite, and we can move on," we have made an exception. These smaller battles make or break our discipline. If we consciously work on them and keep winning those smaller battles, discipline becomes our second nature. After a point, we no longer need to think about it, as choosing the right side of our personality becomes a natural response. It feels effortless because we have developed the skill of discipline by consistently working on it, and ensuring that in all circumstances, we side with what is right, not what is easy.

The ability to withstand temptation and continuously do what needs to be done is the hallmark of a disciplined person. It is not surprising to see those people also being labelled as successful in whichever area they chose to excel. It's being true to your task, making honest choices, and committing to something which is important that helps you succeed. Those who can't do this are the ones who always blame external forces for the situation they are in, but the reality is, they lacked the courage to take a firm stand against the temptations around them.

The big question is: what is the difference between people who display discipline and those who don't? It all boils down to a few fundamental things. The first is the ability to look at the big picture and knowing how not sticking to a plan can ruin that dream of yours. Those who are passionate about the future they are creating don't succumb to temptations. The second is controlling your mind. For the average, weak-

THE ABILITY TO WITHSTAND TEMPTATION AND CONTINUOUSLY DO WHAT NEEDS TO BE DONE IS THE HALLMARK OF A DISCIPLINED PERSON

willed person, every other thought is of giving in to the temptation; they don't even consider the repercussions of their actions. Those who can pause, reflect, and remind themselves of the long-term impact of their thoughts, feelings, and behaviours are the ones who control their actions and act in a disciplined manner. The third aspect is your ability to delay gratification and experience the happiness that comes from self-control. Every time you resist veering off track and stay on course, it is a reminder of your steely self-control. And the belief that you will accomplish what you set out to do, acts as a reward in itself to most of us.

But how do you practice discipline in day-to-day life when there are so many temptations?

1. **Rewire your mind**: The very definition of discipline is doing something less pleasant than the alternatives you have. It's hard work, and it's not easy. Let your mind understand it. Fundamentally, you need to tell yourself that if you have to be productive, then you need to be comfortable with the tasks that are unpleasant and don't come naturally to you. Once you've wired yourself this way, then your mind will support you in the moments of weakness by helping you make better choices. Since you have already told yourself that it's not easy, it becomes more acceptable. Setting the expectation of facing tough choices is the starting point for making these choices.

2. **Remember the marshmallow**: The Stanford Marshmallow Test—led by psychologist Walter Mischel, a professor at Stanford University in 1970—showed us that people who could delay their impulses were far more successful in life and led a life of character and dignity. This experiment

is significant from the perspective of building discipline where immediate gratification achieved through the deviations from a set path leads to low self-control, which in turn hampers progress. Those who want to build a disciplined life should remind themselves that they are cultivating a skill that will make them successful in the long term, leading a fulfilling life that most desire but are unaware how to achieve.

3. **Do things bit by bit:** We should remember that any habit is built gradually, and any big problem needs to be broken down into smaller ones. Trying to tackle everything at once can be detrimental to our effort of achieving larger goals. I remember my experience with running. When I decided to run a marathon, my coach instructed me to wake up at 5 a.m. every day and remind myself that there is a marathon to be run. That reinforcement was important for my mind, as it prepared me for the bigger goal ahead.

    Once I was comfortable with waking up early, I gradually began running—just a few minutes and a few meters at first, but I made sure to follow this schedule religiously, with no compromises. Although in small chunks, but I was able to do it. What the coach helped me do was break down my large goal to small achievable goals, and once I started achieving those goals, my self-confidence started to improve and it prompted me to aim higher. The feeling of being on the right track, following the routine without fail, and not burdening the mind with the enormity of the task at hand is the right way to instill discipline.

4. **Stay committed:** The idea of not giving up and being persistent on the track is important to becoming disciplined. You are on a task and you're focusing on it, then that's

good, but if it requires you to take a break and recharge your batteries, please do so. This isn't a deviation, in fact, it is a strategy to remind yourself that you are preparing for the bigger battle ahead. Sometimes you may falter, but accepting it and getting back on track is the key. Don't let one exception become a reason for other exceptions, but ensure it is used as a reminder of the things you will miss if you don't stay on course.

5. **Learn to forgive yourself**: People who have trouble with discipline are likely continue to face trouble—it's only human. What needs to be thought through is that at least the person is trying. Missing one day of exercise doesn't mean that the journey is over. You can always pick yourself up and make up for the lost time. So what you were not able to stick to the plan this time; pick yourself up and ensure you do what you said you will do.

Discipline can be tough to develop, as it requires huge effort from our side. But once it becomes our second nature, like how Virat Kohli had said while sharing his experience, then we can expect good results, which is worth much more than the sacrifices we made along the way.

5

Grit

Standing Up After Every Fall, Until Everyone
Acknowledges You're Standing Tall

**"OVER TIME, GRIT IS WHAT SEPARATES
FRUITFUL LIVES FROM AIMLESSNESS."**

—JOHN ORTBERG, American author

What is grit? Is it courage, or is it tenacity? Some dictionaries define grit as 'firmness of character' or 'indomitable spirit,' while others argue that it's simply another word for perseverance. It is perhaps hard to describe grit in a single sentence, however, there can never be any doubt that it has been considered as one of the most valued virtues since time immemorial.

There are countless stories of determined sportspersons defying all odds to become accomplished in their fields. Most of the time, the media focuses on stories of 'talented' individuals who go through struggles and then make memorable comebacks. However, we rarely encounter stories of the non-glamorous and 'seemingly not very gifted' players who truly embody the rare and unique virtue of grit in a way that even star sportspersons cannot match. In recent times, perhaps no one can match the story of middle-order batsman Hanuma Vihari whose middle name might as well be 'gritty'!

In 2011, the Indian cricket team had won the ICC Cricket World Cup at home after a gap of 28 years. The very next year, the India Under-19 team won the World Cup in Australia (Townsville, Queensland). The 2012 triumphant batch was hailed as the next big thing in Indian cricket, and it was even argued that 2015 ODI World Cup title looked more attainable because some of these rising stars were expected to be a part of the senior team in a couple of years. Forget 2015, none of the players from that celebrated batch could make it to the senior Indian team, even in the subsequent World Cups in 2019 in England or the latest one in 2023 in India.

Some of the brightest cricketers, such as left-arm spinner Harmeet Singh or skipper Unmukt Chand, failed to make a mark for their respective domestic teams. Even the likes of Vijay Zol and Baba Aparajith, who seemed destined to play for India after their U-19 heroics, couldn't make it, except Hanuma Vihari. Ironically, Vihari wasn't considered good enough for that U-19 World Cup squad until another player Manan Vohra missed out due to a thumb injury. The Andhra player got a call to join the international Indian cricket team in the middle of an ongoing Test series in England in 2018; this marked his India debut in the highest format of the game (Test cricket). It was his natural grit which had kept his optimism alive all these years even as many of his teammates were drifting away.

The biggest reason for Vihari's breakthrough was his persevering nature and an ever-optimistic attitude towards life. He was never distracted or discouraged by the fact that no one from his state had played for India since 1999, as his team wasn't considered strong enough to attract the attention of national selectors. Unfazed by any negative talks, Vihari continued doing what he did best—scoring runs season after season—until everyone had no choice but to notice him. He was averaging nearly 60 runs in first-class cricket, and it was impossible to ignore his candidature.

After his debut in The Oval, Vihar's next match was in Perth, Australia. He had barely established himself in the team, and in the third match of his career, he was asked to open the innings in front of a partisan crowd of over 85,000 at the famous Melbourne Cricket Ground on Boxing Day. The role was not only unusual or tough, but the occasion demanded a gritty player to face a hostile Australian pace attack on the first morning of the Test.

Displaying his typical grit and summoning all his potential power, Vihari managed to blunt the Australian bowling attack for nearly 19 overs. Vihari scored only eight runs from 66 deliveries, but his effort drew special mention from captain Virat Kohli and coach Ravi Shastri as India went on to win both the match and the Test series. There were many splendid contributions from the other high-profile players, but Vihari's resolute display was crucial to India's first-ever Test series win in Australia. It was also due to his grit that Vihari managed to keep the flamboyant and seemingly more talented Rohit Sharma from the red-ball cricket on more than one occasions in his short career.

And if anyone thought that Vihari's gritty display was just a fluke, then let's go back to another Australian tour in 2020-21. India had lost the first match of a four-match series in Adelaide, being infamously bundled out for just 36 runs in the second innings of the pink-ball Test. The then captain of the Indian team, Virat Kohli, had returned to India leaving the reins in the hands of the stand-in captain Ajinkya Rahane. India incredibly won the next Test in Melbourne, largely due to the good performance by Rahane. However, it was the third Test match in Sydney which was tantalizingly poised until the last hour of the final day of a five-day game. From the dominant position of winning the match easily, as long as Rishabh Pant was batting—he made a sparkling 97 runs in a seemingly impossible pursuit of chasing 400-plus in the 4th innings of a Test on Australian soil—India soon found itself battling to save the match as wickets kept tumbling.

Then came Vihari's turn. He was not fit enough to bat, and yet he faced 161 balls and stayed in the middle for more than 50 overs—over 40 of those with a torn hamstring—to help India secure a much-needed result, which was a draw. "Two feelings came to mind. One was pain, the other was relief. The pain was there, and there was also a sigh of relief that I could do the job for the team. It was sweet pain," said Vihari on being asked how was he feeling when he was limping up the stairs at The Sydney Cricket Ground after saving the Test. "That's the kind of feeling I got. I would say for all the years of hard work I had done in first-class cricket, there were no people watching me play and I still had to go through the grind and struggle. And today I had 1.3 billion people back home and across the globe watching me save a Test match... this is what I thought at that moment. The real satisfaction of going through the grind in the first-class arena and then achieving this today was really amazing," explained Vihari in an interview with *ESPNcricinfo. com*[1] after exhibiting one of the finest match-saving innings in the history of Indian cricket. If there are any learnings from

---

[1] "'I Knew It Was the End of My Series; Whatever Impact I'd Have, It Had to Be Then.'" ESPNcricinfo, January 21, 2021. https://www.espncricinfo. com/story/aus-vs-ind-hanuma-vihari-i-knewit- was-the-end-of-my-series-whatever-impact-i-d-have-it-had-to-bethen- 1248681.

Vihari's valour, it has to be his gritty nature that always refused to accept failure.

Vihari has played just 16 Tests (as of January 2025), but remarkably 12 of those have featured him for the tougher overseas assignments. Traditionally, even the best of the Indian batters struggle to achieve similar kind of success in foreign pitches, however, the then 28-year-old Vihari made grit his unique selling point, which helped him establish himself in a team full of brilliant stroke players.

What Is Grit?

A study by *U.S. News & World Report*[2] reveals that nearly 80% of people who make New Year's resolutions fail to keep them. In fact, the majority drop out by the second month. While many begin with a lot of enthusiasm and determination, along the way, they lose motivation and momentum, and simply give up. There are a few, however, who don't. Not only do they stick to their resolutions but also achieve their objectives. Hanuma Vihari's story exemplifies this remarkable determination.

Angela Duckworth, a renowned American psychologist, calls this aspect of personality 'grit'. By definition, grit is not giving up on your goals despite obstacles and hardships. It involves demonstrating perseverance and passion for your goal and determination to stay the course despite difficulties.

Imagine this: you love good food that tastes divine but it's not good for your body. You're on a diet and have promised

---

[2] Most people fail to achieve their new year's resolution. | inc.com. Accessed October 24, 2024. https://www.inc.com/marla-tabaka/why-set-yourself-up-for-failure-ditch-new-years-resolution-do-this-instead.html.

yourself to not eat such food, no matter the temptation. Your self-discipline is tested when the food is presented at different occasions. Now, if you combine this self-discipline with a goal you are chasing and desperately want

to achieve, you will be able to control your urges to indulge yourself. This abstinence then becomes a form of grit, where you are pursuing your goal with perseverance and passion, despite temptations and obstacles.

Simply put, grit is your ability to stay the course despite obstacles. It's hard, yet it has a profound impact. Sometimes the temptation comes in the form of your natural instincts. You know that you play in a certain manner but you give that up because you know it will lead to your downfall. The command on what you will and will not do, given the goal you have, defines grit for you.

Angela Duckworth tells us that grit is a stronger predictor of success in life than intelligence. Her much-celebrated work in this area has proven that West Point U.S. Military Academy cadets who scored higher on grit scale are 60% more likely to complete the tough military training in comparison to those who scored lower. These cadets go through a rigorous program that tests their character and prepares them as a leader in the U.S. Army.

Similarly, Ivy League graduates with higher grit scores secured higher GPAs compared to those with higher IQs. When we compare two individuals with the same backgrounds and intelligence, the one with higher grit will be better educated.

The list goes on and one thing is certain: people with higher levels of grit have a greater probability of being successful, even if they start with lower intelligence or hail from a disadvantaged background. Look at the inspiring stories from the Indian Premier League, where the likes of Mohammed Siraj, T. Natarajan, Chetan Sakariya, Rinku Singh, Yashasvi Jaiswal, Sarfaraz Khan, and many others have proven that courage, tenacity, optimism, and the attitude of never giving up can work wonders in life. Essentially, this underlines the importance of grit.

Time and again, it is understood that building grit is the best investment for anyone seeking to lead a successful and fulfilling life. Look no further than another stalwart of Indian cricket: Cheteshwar Pujara. The Rajkot batsman isn't your typical star who will mesmerize you with his breath-taking shot-making skills like Rohit Sharma or Virat Kohli in white-ball format. However, Pujara, like his idol Rahul Dravid (another gritty cricketer who famously carved a niche for himself in a team full of stars like Sachin Tendulkar, V.V.S. Laxman, Sourav Ganguly, and Virender Sehwag), accomplished something which Sharma could not. Pujara is among India's top 10 all-time great batsmen in Test cricket, a dream for any budding cricketer of his generation, unlike the current generation, which idolizes the performers of T20 format.

> **TIME AND AGAIN, IT IS UNDERSTOOD THAT BUILDING GRIT IS THE BEST INVESTMENT FOR ANYONE SEEKING TO LEAD A SUCCESSFUL AND FULFILLING LIFE**

Rohit Sharma's relative lack of success in Test cricket is often attributed to the lack of grit in his approach, and admirably, Sharma himself has admitted this and started working on it. The fact that Rohit Sharma emerged as India's best batsman in the 2021 England series by embracing grit turned many of his fiercest critics into admirers. (He was the highest run-scorer for the side, scoring 368 runs in four Tests at an average of 52.57, including his maiden overseas Test hundred during the series as an opener.)

OFTEN, WE SUCCUMB TO TEMPTATIONS BECAUSE THEY PROVIDE INSTANT GRATIFICATION

Building grit is important; it is difficult but not impossible. Often, we succumb to temptations because they provide instant gratification. In the quest of feeling that short-term happiness, we forget about the long-term impact of giving in to that temptation. People who remind themselves of their goals and the reasons for their sacrifices have a better chance of developing grit. Rohit Sharma, with his abundant talent to play incredible shots, in the early phase of his Test career succumbed to the temptation of scoring easily and quickly in the red-ball format. While this method worked in white-ball cricket formats, the highest form of the game (Test Series) forced him to be gritty, which he very well demonstrated on the tour of England in 2021 and during the latter phase of his Test career. It was then he earned the respect as an all-format legend.

We all know that being gritty is not easy, then why do some people demonstrate more grittiness than others? According to us, there are a few factors that help them do this, and we can cultivate grit by following these principles in our lives:

1. **A strong motive for the goal**: Pursuing something which is worth pursuing is the cornerstone of why someone shows grit. It depends on how badly you need something and what sacrifices you are willing to make in order to get there. There's no better example than that of Sachin Tendulkar, who was past his prime by 2005, yet kept going. He continued to improve and evolve, not letting his ego get in the way when he was being outplayed by much younger bowlers or getting embarrassed by awkward dismissals. It would have been easier for Tendulkar to walk away gloriously, avoiding those uncomfortable moments, knowing his greatness was beyond any doubt. Yet, he kept chasing higher goals. In his younger days, while it was his natural talent that mesmerized fans and experts, it was his grit that led him to finally win the ultimate World Cup trophy in 2011, after five previously failed attempts.

2. **Sticking to a process**: Success is never accidental. Time and again, life has shown us that you may get lucky once or twice, however, true success comes when you are ready to sweat and give everything to your goal. There may be distractions along the way, but if you are committed to sticking to the process, these distractions won't have any effect on you. Sticking to a process to build habits goes a long way in displaying grit.

3. **Celebrating small successes**: Rome wasn't built in a day, and neither are good habits. We need to understand that our minds are built to be distracted. For us to control it, we must go against our natural tendencies. If someone is able to do it regularly, then they should be rewarded for it. These rewards go a long way in confirming two things: first, the task is worth its weight, and second, the wiring in the brain for the habit is strong.

4. **Track your progress**: Sometimes looking backwards to assess how far we have come reassures us that we are on the right track. Achieving and recognizing milestones and communicating that to our mind helps us understand that we are heading in the right direction.

5. **Building gritty habits:** One of the key aspects that allows you to repeat a behaviour is when you experience the pleasure associated with the reward, which comes after performing that action. While developing grit, we need to reward our brain for the small gains we make. The ability to resist an urge and then rewarding yourself goes a long way in building the grit muscle. Once you see that a particular technique is helping you develop grit, continue with it, and turn it into a habit.

Our lives are defined by the goals we set and the efforts we put into achieving them. We all have a lot of talent and the intent to achieve our goals, but what most of us lack is an unwavering focus to stay the course. Grit is the quality that allows us to pursue our goals without any distractions. Even when times are tough, knowing that we must stick to our plans if we want to achieve a larger goal without getting distracted, means we have developed grit. Without grit, you can't be great!

Like courage, grit is impossible to measure, however, this is a priceless quality to have in our character. The supremely gritty aren't those who fear failure; rather, they embrace it as a part of the process and evolution. Unless we are gritty, it is difficult to understand or appreciate the valuable lessons we may find in defeat.

SECTION II

MANAGING RELATIONSHIPS

6

Empathy

Putting Yourself in Others' Shoes and Feeling Exactly What They Feel

"THE GREATEST GIFT OF HUMAN BEINGS IS THAT WE HAVE THE POWER OF EMPATHY."

—MERYL STREEP, American actress

Our daily newspapers are filled with bad news and chaos. It's disturbing to see the amount of negativity that surrounds us. We are led to believe that people have become callous and are bent on spreading their anger, hatred, and negativity in society. Well, this happens for two reasons: first, negativity attracts attention and makes us take notice of things we normally don't observe; second, these behaviours are not in line with how humans naturally behave, so they are highlighted. Science tells us that as humans, we are programmed to support, understand, and help one another. Probably this aspect of human character has ensured our survival, while species stronger than us have perished.

Empathy is the trait that allows us to do this. It enables us to put ourselves in others' shoes and feel what they are feeling. It's a quality that makes us humane. Our ability to understand the pain, suffering, and challenges of others and our instinct to do everything in our capacity to help them makes us special. The word empathy comes from Greek translation of the word, *empatheia*, which in turn is derived by a German word, *Einfühlung*, meaning "feeling into" someone or something. This derivation makes it clear that fully tuning into someone else's thoughts and feelings is an integral part of displaying empathy.

A question may arise: as humans, we strive to compete and assert our superiority in everything we do, what value does empathy provide in that context? Well, empathy plays an interesting role in helping us build trust and form close relationships. As a leader, you understand that everything can't be done alone and you need a team to help you achieve your desired goals. A team can be built by onboarding people with great skills, but the members within the team won't get along well if they aren't empathetic towards each other where everyone feels for one another and wants the group to succeed collectively.

Take the example of the 2022 Asia Cup champion—the Sri Lankan cricket team. Before the tournament started in September, almost everyone had written them off, and Bangladesh's cricket director had publicly mocked them saying, "I don't think they have any world-class bowlers" ahead of their Asia Cup clash. However, the Sri Lankan team wasn't enraged by these comments because they had arrived in the United Arab Emirates amidst a huge financial turbulence their nation was facing. The players had witnessed food and fuel shortages and other hardships which their friends and family members were facing. The sense of empathy towards each other and citizens of their country galvanized the Sri Lankan team to play as a determined team in the same way they had done it back when they had defied all the odds to become world champions in 1996. Drawing inspiration from that historical victory, Sri Lanka played as a focussed unit, without being dependent on individual performances to win games.

It didn't matter to them that they were missing Dushmantha Chameera, a key figure in their bowling attack. The Lankan victory inspired everyone beyond the 22-yard as Anand Mahindra, Chairman of Mahindra Group, went on to applaud publicly on X:

> "And let me add this morning that Team Sri Lanka is my #MondayMotivation because of their teamwork, which I mentioned, but also because of the way they rose like a Phoenix after a first, demoralising loss to Afghanistan. Their spirit stayed unbroken. https://t.co/nMoO8As4sI
>
> — ANAND MAHINDRA (@anandmahindra) September 12, 2022

Not only Mahindra but a lot of corporate leaders draw inspiration on team-building and unity from sports.

Empathy was key to MS Dhoni's past success and it is the same quality that made Rohit Sharma a more effective leader than Virat Kohli. While some are born with great talent and can perform well independently, in a team, however, individual excellence is of no use if it is not aligned with and inclusive of the team's needs. And this isn't a criticism of Kohli, rather an observation that under Rohit Sharma's leadership Indian dressing room looked calmer and composed.

During Ravi Shastri-Kohli era (coach and captain from

2016 to 2021), there was a perception that great players like Cheteshwar Pujara, Ajinkya Rahane, and Ravichandran Ashwin were subtly sidelined. And they did air their concerns later on, although not directly taking a dig at their captain. However, the way Dinesh Karthik and Hardik Pandya spoke about Rohit Sharma's style of leadership, one could easily sense that Sharma's famous trait—empathy—was winning hearts of his teammates and creating a healthier environment in the team's dressing room.

Another aspect of being empathetic is that it helps you become tolerant of others' behaviour. It helps you understand why someone behaves in a particular way, and instead of reacting, you approach the situation calmly. If a person seems aloof and is not mingling with you doesn't mean they are arrogant or have an attitude, it may also mean that they are suffering and don't know how to cope. An empathetic view allows you to look at the situation from their perspective, to listen to them, understand what they are going through and then take appropriate action to ensure that person returns to being normal. This approach of handling a situation builds trust and results in lifelong partnership or relationship. That's what Dhoni did with Ravindra Jadeja, Ishant Sharma, Suresh Raina, and countless others and what Rohit Sharma has been doing with Suryakumar Yadav, Harshal Patel, and many other players.

At times, empathy also helps you find solutions for others by clearly understanding what will work and what won't. It can also be a part of your overall strategy to create a unique culture around you. Take, for instance, in Indian cricket team, fast bowlers were considered a secondary choice to spinners, and were asked to bowl when spinners were not in action.

When Virat Kohli took over the reins, he wanted to change this culture and started paying more attention to fast bowlers. He understood their problems, workload, and challenges by being around, listening to them, and providing them with the emotional support they needed. This resulted into a formidable pace attack (a group of fast bowlers) that won many matches for India.

AT TIMES, EMPATHY ALSO HELPS YOU FIND SOLUTIONS FOR OTHERS BY CLEARLY UNDERSTANDING WHAT WILL WORK AND WHAT WON'T

Leaders can empathize in contrasting ways, too. There is no one-size-fits-all kind of approach to empathy.

Small gestures by leaders go a long way in building trust. People begin to understand that you are there to take care of them because you understand them. It's a well-known story that on long flights MS Dhoni used to give away his business class seat to his fast bowlers so that they could be well-rested. No one asked him to do it, but this immense sense of empathy and generosity by Dhoni towards his players further strengthened his bond with them. Similarly, Kohli had once visited Mohammad Siraj's home in Hyderabad to eat biryani with his family. The bowler had initially offered to bring home-cooked biryani to the team hotel for his captain. He didn't expect that a high-profile celebrity like Kohli will instead visit his home.

In life and in sports, you win some and you lose some. A great player is the one who doesn't get too excited by wins or too gutted by defeats. An ordinary player is so immersed in personal victories and defeats that they forget that for every winning team, there is a losing team, too. For every player who becomes a hero, there are players who will be labelled

IN LIFE AND IN SPORTS, YOU WIN SOME AND YOU LOSE SOME

as villains or nemesis by teams or fans. A player who is sensitive about the ebbs and troughs displays the sign of a true sportsperson and a good human being. When India lost the World Test championship match in Southampton (England) in 2021, Kane Williamson came over to comfort Virat Kohli—a great example of an empathic leader. Williamson didn't just enjoy his victory but also became a part of Kohli's mental state, who had just lost an opportunity to win a ICC trophy for himself and India, and was in great mental pain. Similarly, when an all-conquering Australia lost a tightly fought Ashes series in 2005 after nearly two decades, the iconic image of the series that remained was of Brett Lee being consoled by Andrew Flintoff (England's Ashes Talisman).

Empathy is basically a natural reaction of our mirror neurons, which allow us to mirror the mood and emotions of those who are around us. This is easy unless we start creating boundaries and not identify the other like us, on the basis of caste, creed, religion, geography, language, and beliefs. The moment you start seeing others as different, our mirror neurons stop firing, and you become unemphatic. As human beings, we are bestowed with the ability of thinking that, at the end of the day, we are dealing with

YOU CAN BE COMPETITIVE BUT YOU CAN ALSO DISPLAY EMPATHY

another human being, who might be representing a different team or different ideology but is similar to us; empathy organically follows. You can be competitive but you can also display empathy.

There are a few things we can do to improve our empathy:

1. **Work on listening skills:** We may hear others, but we might not listen to them. Real connection happens when the other person actively listens to you and makes you believe that they are with you whatever the situation may be. That is what made John Wright (former opening batter of New Zealand) and Gary Kirsten (former South African opening batter) great coaches. Despite coming from diverse backgrounds, they became lifelong friends to many Indian players.

2. **Pay attention to body language:** Sometimes, people don't say how they feel, but their tone and body language reveals a lot about the state they are in. You should be able to understand this. A great leader picks up on these cues and and befriends their players. Ashish Nehra of Gujarat Titans is the best example. Nehra displayed this trait in his first stint as head coach of the new IPL team in 2022 and led them to IPL championship in their very first season in the same year.

3. **Try to understand others, even when you disagree with them:** It's okay for people to have different opinions. Merely having a different opinion doesn't make them your enemy. Your ability to appreciate their point of view and perspective may help you refine your own thought process and develop empathy. Former Australian coach John Buchanan exemplified this. He was regularly

ridiculed by a legend like Shane Warne who wasn't fond of a structured way of coaching. Rather than fighting with Warne, Buchanan empathized with Warne's vision and adopted changes to his coaching techniques.

4. **Ask questions:** We often form opinions about others based on hearsay or unverified information. Hardly do we delve deeper into why someone says something. Asking them questions can reveal a lot about them and their perspective. Seeking answers without any bias builds empathy and forms deeper connection with the person. This makes you understand why someone said something or did a particular thing.

5. **Imagine yourself in someone else's shoe:** It's easy to criticize and castigate someone but harder to understand the perspective of others. Imagine a debutant walking in to bat or bowl and being gripped by nervousness. A great leader ensures that such young players are able to stay calm and motivated because they know what it feels like making a debut in such a competitive environment.

   Sourav Ganguly displayed this virtue during his successful tenure with the Indian cricket team in the beginning of the new century. Ganguly, who was dismissed and side-lined after just one match for several years, made it a point that he would give enough chances to any new player before they can be left out from the scheme of things. Ganguly's backing of Virender Sehwag, Yuvraj Singh, and Harbhajan Singh during their initial years on the field is a testimony to that. This allowed them to first settle as players of the Indian cricket team, and later on, helped them in honing their skills and become great sportsmen.

Empathy is a great quality to possess because it not only allows us to form deeper connections with others but also makes us humane. We can be successful and still lead a melancholic life if we don't have empathy. At the end of the day, it's the relationships that bring the most joy in life, says a Harvard study[1]. If you don't have people who root for you through thick and thin, then you don't have a life where happiness comes to you through relationships. Empathy can surely be the panacea for situations like this and help you build meaningful relationships.

---

[1] Gazettemikepetroff. "Over Nearly 80 Years, Harvard Study Has Been Showing How to Live a Healthy and Happy Life." Harvard Gazette, January 11, 2024. https://news.harvard.edu/gazette/story/2017/04/over-nearly-80-years-harvard-study-has-been-showing-how-to-live-a-healthy-and-happy-life/.

7

Emotional Intelligence

Understanding Emotions of Self, Understanding Emotions of Others

"WHEN AWARENESS IS BROUGHT TO AN EMOTION, POWER IS BROUGHT TO YOUR LIFE."

—TARA MEYER ROBSON, a mind-body-life expert and the creator of The Flow Method

Human beings are different and special from the rest of the species on this planet. They can think, analyze, and often chose their response. This is because they have a brain that allows them to process data instantly and then make choices. Of course, it requires tremendous effort from human beings to ensure that the system works as it is supposed to.

Why Is that?

It is because, apart from the analytical skills, human beings also have emotions and feelings. Broadly, emotions are defined as a state of consciousness in which various internal sensations are experienced by humans. These emotions can be triggered by a thought, memory, or something present in the external environment. These emotions may alter our physical state and encourage or provoke us to act in a certain way. Emotions significantly impact our choices and behaviours. Unless we manage them properly, they overpower us and affect our logical thinking, putting us in danger of doing something we should not do.

The ability to regulate your emotions is what EQ (Emotional Quotient) is all about. EQ helps us understand, use, and manage our emotions in a positive way to relieve our stress, help us communicate effectively, empathize with others, overcome challenges, and diffuse conflicts. If we can do all of this, we are likely to lead a balanced life, where the positive regulation of emotions leads to what researchers call a thriving and successful life.

Sachin Tendulkar, Virat Kohli, and Rishabh Pant—what do they have in common? You may say Tendulkar was arguably India's greatest batsman, Kohli has been his true successor, and Pant is now regarded as once-in-a-generation talent. However, there is something more that connects them. All of them have exhibited incredible emotional intelligence under severely challenging circumstances. What could be more emotionally challenging than playing cricket for your country, state, or your IPL team immediately after the death of your father? Tendulkar lost his father in 1999 when he was playing in the World Cup. He returned from England to attend the funeral, then took the next flight back to England and scored a century. In the winter of 2007, Kohli lost his father early in the morning but went on to play a match-saving innings for his state (Delhi) in a Ranji Trophy game against Karnataka, returning for his father's funeral in the evening.

Nearly a decade later, Pant was going through a similar kind of grief when he played an IPL match for Delhi Daredevils in April 2017. After performing the last rites of his father, who had passed away in Roorkee, Pant returned to the pitch and scored a 50 against Royal Challengers Bangalore. These instances evoked those memories of Tendulkar and Kohli. While it may have been their way of distracting themselves from the unbearable loss, their decision to play despite this speaks volumes about their mental resolve and ability to manage emotions in an unusual way.

While EQ is an extremely important skill to develop, it also helps us build and maintain relationships, achieve our goals constructively, and respond to difficult situations in life. This trait is essential for a successful career in the sporting world.

Competitive and professional sports, by their very nature, often put athletes in stressful situations. The ability of the person to absorb that stress without losing their mental balance and do what they are supposed to do is tested every moment. It requires great self-awareness, self-management, social awareness, and, in team games, the ability to manage relationships. If you are unaware of the emotional state you are in, you will make mistakes.

In 1986, former India pacer Chetan Sharma famously

COMPETITIVE AND PROFESSIONAL SPORTS, BY THEIR VERY NATURE, OFTEN PUT ATHLETES IN STRESSFUL SITUATIONS

buckled under pressure in front of Pakistani batsman Javed Miandad who hit him for a last-ball six in an ODI Australasia Cup final match between arch rivals Indian and Pakistan. Even though Sharma had played a good three years of international cricket with nearly 30 ODIs under his belt, he was in awe of Javed Miandad. The Pakistani batsman was notorious for his ploy of sledging and defeating his rivals with his remarks. Miandad knew that the match would go in the last over and even if Chetan Sharma was the most successful bowler of the match (with three wickets to his name), he could sense that Sharma was likely to succumb under pressure. And he did. Sharma bowled the easiest last ball (a full toss, which is considered easy to hit a six) and the rest is history. It was such a huge psychological blow to the Indian mindset that Pakistan continued to dominate India in the cricket arena for the next two decades.

Contrast this with the 2007 ICC World Twenty20 final in Johannesburg in South Africa, where a lesser-known Joginder Sharma was bowling to Pakistan's Misbah-ul-Haq who was anchoring the Pakistani innings smoothly, and it seemed that last over was mere a formality. The pressure on Joginder Sharma was enormous, but he didn't blink. He did not have any great experience of international cricket at the time and not much was expected from him, yet he kept his cool. His bowling forced Misbah-ul-Haq to make a mistake and the ball landed safely in the hands of Sreesanth at fine leg. His captain, MS Dhoni, later revealed that he had seen Joginder Sharma handle similar stressful situations in Delhi club games, which gave him confidence in his teammate to pull this off. The last over gamble was as much a classic exhibition of Dhoni's coolness as it was Joginder Sharma's EQ. It is easy to get carried away or lose focus in high-stakes Indo-Pak games, but to keep one's emotion in check requires enormous self-awareness.

WHILE EMOTIONS COME NATURALLY TO US, EMOTIONAL INTELLIGENCE CAN BE DEVELOPED

While emotions come naturally to us, emotional intelligence can be developed. Some players may be born with it, but others develop it over time as they go through challenging situations. An ordinary player crumbles under pressure, but a great player never lets their emotions get the best of them, understands what needs to be done, and then does exactly that.

Winning an IPL trophy is arguably one of the toughest tasks for a IPL team captain. Even Dhoni is not the most successful captain in this format, and Virat Kohli, despite leading RCB for nearly a decade, never managed to win the trophy. However, Hardik Pandya, in his very first stint as Gujarat Titans' captain, led his team remarkably and won the title. Pandya had no prior experience of captaincy, not even at the Ranji Trophy or club level, but his EQ was his biggest strength. Each member of his squad spoke glowingly about Pandya's calmness under stress and his ability to bring the team together with his cheerful personality.

Gujarat Titans' Spinner Sai Kishore mentioned during an interview with *CricketNext* how Pandya and Dhoni are similar when it comes to keeping their cool as captains and handling stressful situations. "They both are pretty calm in challenging situations, that helps to maintain positive environment in a team. One thing I really admired about Hardik was his ability to handle his success and failure in equal measure. That is a unique quality about Hardik, he's a pretty level-headed person and that works for him," Kishore added.

As a leader, your ability to get the best out of your team requires you to not only understand your emotional state but also the emotions of those around you. You need to empathize with the person, understand their context, and allow them to express themselves in their own comfortable way.

One of the distinctive features of a great leader is the ability to show tremendous EQ for themselves before they apply the same technique on those around them. It shouldn't come as a surprise that despite limited resources, players with higher EQ are able to bring out the best in their teammates.

Dealing with profound grief in a mature way (like Tendulkar, Kohli, and Pant) is perhaps an illustration of a high emotional intelligence. While not everyone may possess such a high level of maturity, it's certainly a skill that can and should be learned by anyone who wants to succeed in life. The big question is, how do you develop it?

Here are some practical ways in which EQ can be developed by everyone:

1. **Using negative emotions as learning opportunities:** In life, as in sports, you are bound to feel negative emotions. Your ability to acknowledge them, see the bigger picture, and accept them as a learning experiences to improve yourself is a first step towards developing a good EQ.

2. **Practicing empathy**: We often want things to happen in a certain way, and we expect others to behave accordingly. When that doesn't happen, we feel angry or frustrated. Showing a little empathy, however, can help us see things from their perspective and develop EQ.

3. **Knowing your triggers and handling them well:** Everyone has different stressors, and exposure to them generates

different reactions. Being aware of what stresses us will give us tremendous insight on handling them and responding better in adverse situations. For example, the thought of attending your weekly Monday morning meeting may trigger stress on Sunday evening itself. Once you recognize this trigger, engage in a self-talk about how well the meeting will go, given the preparation you have put in. Also, remind yourself that in similar situations in the past, how you have always performed well. Self-talks like this can help calm these stressors.

4. **Practicing equanimity:** Often, as humans, we get carried away by victories or defeats, forgetting that all of this is temporary. Things change; neither your bad form or good form will last forever. When you don't rejoice too much in victories and don't dwell unnecessarily on your defeats for long, know that you are developing your emotional intelligence.

5. **Developing a positive mindset:** Challenges are inevitable, and what differentiates great players from the rest is how they can approach those challenges. Your ability to stay positive in difficult circumstances is what helps sharpen your EQ.

Essentially, all the players who represent their country have talent; that's why they are chosen. However, only a handful become legends by ensuring they do things which are difficult over a long period of time and in a sustained manner. What sets them apart from others is their EQ—their ability to understand their emotional state, use it positively to their advantage, and deliver results. Talent may get you there, but it's your EQ that determines whether you truly belong to that place or not.

8

Trust

Believing in Someone More than You Believe in Yourself

"TRUST IS THE GLUE OF LIFE. IT'S THE MOST ESSENTIAL INGREDIENT IN EFFECTIVE COMMUNICATION. IT'S THE FOUNDATIONAL PRINCIPAL WHICH HOLDS ALL RELATIONSHIPS."

—STEPHEN COVEY, American educator and author

What is human life without relationships? Nothing. The longest study on happiness, conducted by Harvard University (as reported by Robert Waldinger and Marc Schulz in their book *The Good Life*) found that strong relationships are one of the most important factors—compared to accomplishments and social status—in predicting the level of happiness a person will experience in life. Without strong relationships, you cannot imagine leading a fulfilling life. And what creates these relationships? Trust.

Trust is perhaps best described as a firm belief that someone is good, honest, and will not harm you. It is a mental state where you believe that someone is safe and reliable. These are the people who do what they say and say what they do—every time.

TRUST IS PERHAPS BEST DESCRIBED AS A FIRM BELIEF THAT SOMEONE IS GOOD, HONEST, AND WILL NOT HARM YOU

So, Why Is Trust So Important in Life?

Because it brings several benefits. When you trust someone, you create what psychologists call 'psychological safety'[1], allowing you to be yourself without fear of negative consequences. Look at the story of Suryakumar Yadav, who made his T20 debut after turning 30. He was always considered a fine batsman, but wasn't fully trusted for his abilities in domestic cricket by his coaches or captains. Even though when he secured an IPL contract with Mumbai Indians in 2011, he only managed to play a few matches until 2013. However, once he was picked by Gautam Gambhir, the captain of Kolkata Knight Riders, in 2014, his career took a decisive turn. Gambhir, as a true leader, backed him to the hilt and allowed him to improvise, innovate, and play fearlessly.

---

[1] Wietrak, E. and Gifford, J. (2024) Trust and psychological safety: An evidence review. Practice summary and recommendations. London: Chartered Institute of Personnel and Development. https://www.cipd.org/globalassets/media/knowledge/knowledge-hub/evidence-reviews/2024-pdfs/8542-psych-safety-trust-practice-summary.pdf

Suryakumar Yadav was a different player now, playing useful cameos lower down the order and featuring in every game of the Kolkata Knight Riders' title-winning campaign in 2014. And, his progress was being noticed by his long-time friend Rohit Sharma, who had started captaining the Mumbai Indians team by then. Rohit Sharma wanted Yadav back in his team. While Gambhir continued to trust Yadav and his methods, some of the coaches and KKR management did not see much value in the youngster, as he managed to score only 684 runs over four seasons (with just one 50-plus score). He was released from the KKR franchise ahead of 2018 mega auction, and Rohit Sharma's trust in Suryakumar Yadav led Mumbai Indians to bid at ₹3.20 crore for the local lad in the 2018 auction.

In the 2018 IPL season, Suryakumar Yadav finished as the highest run-getter in the tournament for Mumbai, with an impressive tally of 512 runs (average 36.57, strike rate 133.33). Since then, he has risen significantly in Indian cricket. After making his T20I debut under Virat Kohli's captaincy, he debuted in ODIs and Tests under Rohit Sharma. He became the first-ever Indian player to make his debut in all formats after turning 30. If Suryakumar Yadav had not been trusted by his captains, he would have been a lost talent like many before him. His remarkable consistency was one of the few bright spots in an otherwise disappointing campaign for the franchise.

Good captains know that players can be trusted with their abilities. Once the psychological safety is created, they express themselves fearlessly on the cricket field. Once trust is established

GOOD CAPTAINS KNOW THAT PLAYERS CAN BE TRUSTED WITH THEIR ABILITIES

between the individuals or organizations, it also ensures that one can take on calculated risks.

In IPL, nothing epitomizes trust better than the bonding between the owner of the Chennai Super Kings (CSK) N. Srinivasan and its captain MS Dhoni. Even when Dhoni was not an icon yet, Srinivasan wanted him to lead CSK at any cost. Despite Dhoni having no connection with Chennai, he was bought in a record bid in 2008 for CSK, and the rest, as they say, is history. Once Dhoni was in the team, Srinivasan trusted him completely and gave him a free hand. Because of this trust, CSK managed to build a system that has continued to deliver results despite various changes and challenges over the years.

Cricket is a team sport, and it inherently requires trust among different players during different phases of the game. For instance, a single converting into double or a double into triple requires trust between two batsmen. They may not talk, but even a simple gesture ensures a mutual understanding of what is required to be done. While the mainstream media may spin stories based on conspiracy theories between superstar players (like Virat Kohli and Rohit Sharma), a closer look at their partnerships—whether playing together or playing under each other's captaincy—displays a certain element of trust which allows them to perform at their best.

It is not true that you can only trust your friends and family members. On the contrary, cricket shows that trusting your colleagues and teammates can significantly impact your career. India's greatest match-winner, Anil Kumble, did not play a single match in the 2003 World Cup in South Africa, despite being senior to spinner Harbhajan Singh who was preferred by captain Sourav Ganguly. Yet, Kumble was never bitter; he never complained nor created any drama that might have affected the team's environment. He trusted his captain's decision, knowing that it was made in the best interest of the team, and not thinking about just one individual. Kumble introspected and improved himself, and eventually ended his career with more international wickets than any other Indian, finishing as the third-highest wicket-taker after Muttiah Muralitharan and Shane Warne among all-time greats.

WHEN YOU ARE SURROUNDED BY PEOPLE WHO TRUST YOU, YOU BECOME MORE OPTIMISTIC AND ARE GEARED TO ACHIEVE POSITIVE RESULTS

When you are surrounded by people who trust you, you become more optimistic and are geared to achieve positive results. You move with an air of certainty because you are aware that everyone in the team is going to do what they are supposed to do. That positivity and trust translates into the field and converts into a great performance.

If trust is so important, then the question arises: what makes some people more trustworthy than others?

The answer is simple. It lies in the way a person views themselves and others around them. More often than not, these people do what they say they will and back up their words with action—not once or twice, but consistently. That level of consistency is what creates trust.

One of India's finest pacers, Mohammed Shami, experienced a significant upheaval in his life and career in March 2018. His then-wife, Hasin Jahan, made sensational allegations of adultery, domestic violence, rape, and match-fixing against him, so much so that not only was an FIR lodged against him but this even forced the Board of Control for Cricket in India (BCCI) to withhold Shami's annual contract. Amidst this turmoil, Shami's captain, Virat Kohli, stood by him. Although Kohli didn't make any public comment (due to his contract with the BCCI, which restricts players from expressing their opinion in public on sensitive matters), he privately assured Shami that his place in the team would not be affected if he were found innocent of any wrongdoing. The controversy dragged on for months, even years, but Shami's on-field performance remained largely unaffected due to the backing he received from his captain and teammates. The trust and bonding among the players played a pivotal role in Shami not losing his way when his public reputation took a severe hit. In January 2023, a Kolkata court ordered Shami to pay a monthly alimony of ₹50,000 to his now estranged wife Hasin Jahan. However, after the court order, Jahan expressed displeasure with the alimony amount, as she had originally demanded ₹10 lakh per month from the Indian pacer.

Another aspect of trustworthy people is the fact that they are honest and don't hide their weaknesses; they will take accountability for their actions and work on it. While that brutal honesty may be difficult to handle at first, it builds trust in the long run. You also trust those who are not driven by personal gains. While no one is a saint, trustworthy individuals ensure that while they pursue their own goals, they also look out for others' interests. Knowing that someone who matters has your back goes a long way in fostering trust. Google's Project Oxygen[2] discovered this after an extensive

---

[2] Jeffrey Pfeffer and Robert I. Sutton. "How Google Sold Its Engineers on Management." Harvard Business Review, May 22, 2023. https://hbr.org/2013/12/how-google-sold-its-engineers-on-management.

research on the importance of managerial behaviours that enhance trust and performance. One key finding stated that employees trust those managers more who deliver difficult feedback constructively. It's not about just giving feedback, but conveying it in a manner in which the person accepts it and sees value in that criticism—and this, in turn, builds trust.

At the core, trustworthy people genuinely care for others and think about rising above personal gains and creating an environment where others can succeed. In great team environments, not just successes, but failures, too, are handled in a mature way.

Despite concerns in the media over the selection of wicketkeeper and batter Dinesh Karthik, bowling all-rounder Ravichandran Ashwin, and fast bowler Bhubaneshwar Kumar for the T20 World Cup in Australia, the selectors and coach (Rahul Dravid) and captain (Rohit Sharma) backed the experienced trio. When Team India failed to reach the final, the captain and coach were heavily criticized for their backing of the senior players who were apparently past their prime. It would have been easy to scapegoat them publicly and avoid the scrutiny, but neither the coach nor the captain did that. They quietly accepted the failure and moved on, as the trio was never picked again for T20 internationals. What they earned from this move, however, was the trust of both the veteran players and the younger ones, who could feel confident that their captain and coach would not abandon them no matter the circumstances. Sometimes, the greatest lessons in life and sports are not found in glittering triumphs, but in the darker moments of shattering loss.

Trusting someone can often give you results, but when it doesn't, that's when you are truly tested. How you treat the person you backed when things don't go well makes a lot of difference to other team members. How you take accountability of the failures while letting the team bask in the glory when everything goes right defines the level of trustworthiness you have created for yourself.

MS Dhoni trusted a young and dynamic Virat Kohli immensely. During India's Australia tour in 2011-12, the team had lost the first two matches embarrassingly, and there was media outrage to drop young Kohli from the next match in Perth. Even Mohinder Amarnath, the chairman of the selection committee, wanted Dhoni to drop Kohli, but Dhoni refused. His argument was that even if India were to lose the next two matches, he would not drop Kohli, who he believed was the future of Indian batting and it would also severely impact the youngster's confidence. Amarnath, at the time, pointed out to Kohli's previous 11 innings, which had yielded just two 50-plus scores and not a single century. This didn't deter Dhoni. In the next seven innings, Kohli scored 44, 75, 116, 22, 58, 103, and 51*(not out), and perhaps even exceeded Dhoni's expectations, as he went on to become one of the legends of the game.

Even when Dhoni retired from the game and rarely spoke to his former teammates, he continued to support Kohli when he was going through the toughest phase in his international career. After emerging as the top-scorer for India against Pakistan in the 2022 Asia Cup, in my capacity as a sports journalist, I (Vimal Kumar) pointedly asked Kohli in a crowded press conference on how he dealt with the lowest phase of his career and who stood by him in this phase. His answer made headlines even in global media when he revealed that the only person who made the effort to reach out to him during his struggles was MS Dhoni. "Let me tell you one thing: when I left Test captaincy, I got a message from only one person, with whom I had played previously; that was MS Dhoni," Kohli said. "Many people have my number. On TV, people give lots of suggestions, they have a lot to say. But none of the people who had my number sent me a message. That respect [with Dhoni], that connection you have with someone, when it is genuine, it shows, because there is no insecurity. Neither does he [Dhoni] need anything from me, nor do I need anything from him."

When you trust someone unconditionally, there may be times when you are bound to feel cheated or taken for granted if they did not behave in the way you expected them to. In these circumstances, your brain sends signals that make you question your decision to trust someone. You need to remind yourself that no two people are the same and you should not generalize the outcomes and be hard on yourself. It is their behaviour, upbringing, and nature which made them do things in a particular manner, and this should not affect the way you think about others. At most, you can be cautious and follow certain principles before placing your complete trust in someone else.

What are these principles? Well, they are quite simple to understand but difficult to follow through:

1. **Start with pure trust:** Believe that the other person is good unless they give you a reason to believe otherwise. Instead of focussing on what could go wrong, think about instances where someone has actually lived up to your trust and feed your mind with that positivity.

2. **Be honest:** Your trust should be genuine. There needs to be an alignment between what you feel, speak, and do. Any asymmetry around these will send a signal to your brain that you are pretending to trust but aren't fully trusting the person.

3. **Be interested in the whole person:** In professional sports, people often come together to achieve a common goal. Everyone in the team has to play a part, and when someone feels trusted, they deliver what's expected of them every time. This happens because the player feels valued, not just as a team player but as a part of the family and beyond. Always ask questions, listen to people attentively, and try to help them achieve what they want to. This attitude fosters trust because it comes from your honest efforts.

4. **Be forgiving:** Sometimes, others may not live up to your expectations, and that's absolutely fine. Instead of berating yourself, you should learn to forgive—both the person who wasn't trustworthy and yourself as you can't be correct all the time. To forgive someone, you need to develop empathy by putting yourself in their shoes and thinking why someone acted in a certain way. This empathy will allow you to see things from their perspective and help you become a more forgiving person. When people see this, they realize that you are not vengeful and operate from a place of love and care, which helps you build trust.

People thrive in trustworthy environments. When performance pressure is high, the trust quotient required needs to increase accordingly. Trust can help people achieve remarkable things. Sometimes, even those who are trusted may not trust themselves, but once the trust is placed on them, they surprise everyone. A trustworthy environment brings out the best in everyone involved. Always remember, one thing that will continue to elevate humanity is our ability to trust each other—forever and always.

9

Courage

Standing up for What Is Right, Today, Tomorrow, and Always

"COURAGE IS THE MOST IMPORTANT OF ALL THE VIRTUES BECAUSE WITHOUT COURAGE, YOU CAN'T PRACTICE ANY OTHER VIRTUE CONSISTENTLY."

—MAYA ANGELOU, American poet and memoirist

There is a famous advertisement for the aerated drink Mountain Dew in which the protagonist (a stunt-biker) is fearful of carrying out a motor stunt. At this critical juncture, as the daunting task confronts him and pushes him to his limits, he thinks: "*Dar sabko lagta hai, gala sab ka sookhta hai. Par dar se daroge to kuch bada kaise karoge? Dar ke aage jeet hai!* (Everyone feels fear; everyone's throat goes dry out of fear. But if we are afraid of fear, how will we achieve anything great? Beyond fear lies victory!)." This advertisement perfectly encapsulates courage.

Even though the actors in the ad have changed over the

years, no one has captured the true essence of the scriptwriter's words than India's most successful captain in men's cricket—Mahendra Singh Dhoni. In that ad, Dhoni speaks about how he overcame the fear of losing a permanent government job if he pursued his passion for cricket. In fact, everyone, including his parents and friends, advised him to play it safe, as government jobs are hard to secure in India, and for a man from a humble background, it was a huge risk to choose cricket at that point in his career. This story is further elaborated in his autobiographical movie *M. S. Dhoni: The Untold Story* (2016).

As a sports journalist covering cricket, I (Vimal Kumar) have had the privilege to witness Dhoni's journey from close quarters and had countless occasions of memorable conversations with the legend—at airports around the world, in luxurious hotels, and, of course, at several cricket stadiums. Yet, Dhoni never spoke of being afraid of anything, which has made him such a great player that he is today. When I spoke to his teammates, they unanimously said: "*Bande main himmat bahut hai warna Jharkhand se India khelna hi kitni badi baat hoti hai, kaptani toh chor hi doh.*" (The man has a lot of courage, how else could someone from Jharkhand even play for India, let alone become a hugely successful captain?) Unfortunately, while eulogizing Dhoni's story, many lazily credited his success to luck, and only a few highlighted the courageous aspect of his personality.

Many researchers, including Dr. Katherine Dahlsgaard, Jordan Peterson, and Martin Seligman, have tried to define this trait, but none have explained the concept as clearly as Brené Brown, a professor at University of Houston and a researcher on power of vulnerability. She defines courage as the ability to face fear and act despite the possibility of failure, rejection, and criticism. According to her, courage is not about the absence of fear; rather it is the willingness to face fear and act anyway. She argues that vulnerability is an essential component of courage, and being open and honest about our fears and struggles can increase our resilience.

So, if we look at courage from this perspective, two components emerge: one, the presence of fear, and second, the persistent action despite that fear. People are fearful of many things, and when that fear overtakes us, our thinking brain shuts shop, causing us to either freeze or prepare to fight. Not giving up and standing up to the challenge despite the fear is what makes us courageous.

In many ways, courage is like having immense self-belief in overcoming any odds. That's why MS Dhoni could trust a rookie like Joginder Sharma for the toughest possible last over in a T20I match. We're talking about the thrilling 2007 ICC World Twenty20 final against Pakistan. Pakistan needed 13 runs from 6 balls and Joginder Sharma had bowled a wide in the first delivery, followed by a dot ball, and then a full toss, to which Misbah-ul-Haq smashed a six leaving Pakistan only six runs short of victory off four balls. It was possible that Joginder Sharma could have given the Pakistani batter Misbah-ul-Haq another six runs. All were apprehensive about Dhoni's bold move of giving Joginder Sharma the last over. However, the next ball delivered by Sharma sealed Pakistan's fate as Haq's scoop shot landed straight into the hands of Sreesanth, handing India the World Cup. That

NOT GIVING UP AND STANDING UP TO THE CHALLENGE DESPITE THE FEAR IS WHAT MAKES US COURAGEOUS

was, undoubtedly, one of the most courageous decisions in cricket captaincy.

"I want to go to war with this guy," former India coach Gary Kirsten famously said that about Dhoni after 2011 World Cup win in India. The former South African opener worked as head coach of Team India for close to four years. Even if Dhoni was a cricketer, he often thought and conducted himself like a soldier. The lack of fear in his personality can be traced back to that mindset.

Another aspect of courage is that it's not related to your physicality, such as the size and relative strength of a human body. As a teenager, Sachin Tendulkar desperately wanted to tour West Indies to face the hostile pace attack of Ian Bishop, Curtly Ambrose, and Courtney Walsh. However, the chairman of selectors and the then coach thought he was too young to face those fearsome pacers, so Tendulkar wasn't picked for that tour of West Indies in 1989. Yet he wanted to prove to the world that he was good enough to face them. That was a sign of courage, and no wonder he ended up as one of the most accomplished batsmen of all time. Tendulkar's childhood hero, Sunil Gavaskar, was famous for his courage on the field, as he never wore a helmet while facing the fiercest pace attack of all-time from the Caribbean, from the early 1970s till the mid-1980s.

Sometimes, the courage **SOMETIMES, THE COURAGE ONE DEMONSTRATES IS PHYSICAL IN NATURE, AND SOMETIMES IT IS OUR MENTAL COURAGE WHICH COMES TO THE FORE** one demonstrates is physical in nature and sometimes it is our mental courage which comes to the fore. But at the end of the day, courage is someone's persistence in doing what is right despite the obstacles. The fear that arises because of bodily pain or facing death is tangible. You can see how a particular situation will have an adverse impact on your body, but despite that, you stand your ground.

We have several examples where despite enormous pain, players have stood up for their teams. One can not forget that moment when former South African opening batsman Gream Smith came out to bat despite having a broken thumb in the third and final match of a series against Australia in Sydney in 2009. During the first innings, Mitchell Johnson's short-pitched delivery hit Smith's gloves, forcing him to retire hurt. Smith didn't bat again until the fall of the ninth wicket in the second innings. Even Anil Kumble had bowled with a broken jaw in the West Indies in 1997. These are examples of people standing up to physical pain and demonstrating courage to do what was required of them.

Then there's moral courage, which deals with others' adverse opinion about you. Looking foolish in front of others is a universal fear, but when you have the moral courage, you stick to doing what is right despite popular opinion. Traditionally known for their conservative take on the game, it was outrageously courageous of England cricket team's ultra-aggressive brand of cricket which won them a World Cup in ODI and T20 cricket. The same philosophy was implemented in Test cricket as well. That England can revolutionize Test cricket with their 'attack all the time' philosophy of their coach Brendon McCullum and captain Ben Stokes was unthinkable. So much so that, just before the all-important Ashes series in early 2023, Stokes publicly declared that they would continue to pursue their bold and fearless brand of cricket, even at the risk of defeat. "I am not going to change anything just because it's the Ashes," said Stokes.

Speaking to *Sky Sports*, Stokes added: "Every game that I play in this Ashes is going to be about forcing a result, and it doesn't matter what the score is, what the situation is. It won't change. That wouldn't be being true to myself. Every player knows that the Ashes is where everything just ramps up a bit, from pressure to exposure, but we'll stick to what we do. I've been around long enough, so I have Baz [McCullum] and our senior players to make sure those little things don't creep into the dressing room," said Stokes which sounded more like an Australian captain who is always seen as the champion of aggressive style of cricket in any format of the game. By April 2023, England had won 10 out of 12 Test matches under captain Stokes and coach Brendon McCullum.

Moral courage arises in several circumstances—whether it is the fear of criticism, fear of losing something which is dear to you, or fear of making enemies. Sometimes, it is also about fear of not being true to yourself which brings out the moral courage as they can't face themselves in the mirror if they don't act in a particular manner. When former South African captain Hansie Cronje revealed that he had taken money from the bookie to fix the result of the matches, he was at the top of the game and under no external pressure to confess. Yet he went ahead, demonstrating moral courage as it would have been difficult for him to live with his conscience. To this date, a lot of his contemporaries from India and Pakistan never admitted of any wrongdoings publicly, despite proven guilty.

No one is born with courage. It takes the right role models, advice, self-reflection, and practice which allows one to develop courage in one's personality. What happens when you see a clerk in the superstore giving you more money in change than what they were supposed to? Do you have the moral courage to say it to them and give back the extra amount? What happens when you see someone behaving inappropriately with others? Do you stand up and say it's wrong? If we look closely, we will find several situations in our daily lives where we can demonstrate courage and encourage ourselves to build our 'courage muscle'. Playing deliveries by bowlers you fear and taking up challenges where you know you are weak are steps to strengthen this muscle.

No one illustrates this better than wicketkeeper-batsman Rishabh Pant. His unorthodox style of batting often raised doubts about his potential success in Test cricket. Pant was stepping into the large shoes of MS Dhoni, but he didn't try to be the next Dhoni. He had an unusual belief in his style that he soon became the India's greatest ever wicketkeeper-batsman despite playing fewer Test matches than Dhoni. If you look at Pant's Test career, he played countless match-winning innings, and was rarely bothered about his personal milestones. Until November 2024, Pant had scored six centuries in 39 Tests, and the figure would have easily been 12 had Pant converted his seven 90s into 100s. But the 27-year-old is unbothered by the conversion rate and said he doesn't care much about the landmarks.

After he got out for 93 on Day 2 of a Test match in Bangladesh, he was asked if the 'nervous 90s' had an impact on him, to which he replied, "As an individual, I don't think about the landmarks so much. Three figures are just a number for me, I try to play for the situation most of the time. If it happens, it's good. If it doesn't, can't control that." This devil-may-care attitude reflects courage, where focussing on team's success over personal milestones is what sets Pant apart from many of his contemporaries.

How to Be Courageous?

In essence, being courageous means acting despite your fears. So, the first step in being courageous is to know and confront your fears. Find the reasons of your fear and dissect them to understand the root cause.

Overcoming fear is one aspect, but doing something challenging repeatedly builds confidence and prepares you for the tougher challenges ahead.

It also important to remember that being courageous doesn't mean that you will be successful all the time in your endeavour; you may naturally encounter failures at some point. How you deal with those failures makes a significant difference to your inner self-talk and confidence. One way of embracing courage is to be comfortable with your failures and accepting it as a learning experience. This attitude of not giving up despite your failures allows you to stand up and demonstrate courage while facing a similar situation in future.

Whether we like it or not, no progress is ever made unless someone shows enough courage to challenge the status quo. On the one hand, it requires an ability to overcome the fear, and, on the other, it's also about having the confidence that you will achieve what you are intending to achieve despite that fear. This confidence eventually grows to an extent that even when you fail, you stand up, revive yourself, and then try another attempt. Humankind has moved forward because of this, and will continue to do so in future as well.

10

Humility

The Mark of True Wisdom Is Knowing That You Don't Know Everything

"TRUE HUMILITY IS NOT THINKING LESS OF YOURSELF; IT IS THINKING OF YOURSELF LESS."

—RICK WARREN, American pastor and author

We live in a world that encourages us to strive hard, achieve goals, and display those achievements for external approval and validation. This gives us a sense of pleasure and makes us happier, but that happiness is short-lived. The pride, however, takes root and inflates our ego. We begin to boast about our achievements as if it's solely our doing. The

TRUTH BE TOLD, IT IS THE CIRCUMSTANCES AROUND US, KNOWINGLY OR UNKNOWINGLY, THAT PLAY A CRUCIAL ROLE IN SHAPING WHO WE BECOME

more we think of ourselves as the only creators of those successful moments, the more we believe that we hold the power to do everything ourselves, the more our pride inflates, and we begin to feel superior. Truth be told, it is the circumstances around us, knowingly or unknowingly, that play a crucial role in shaping who we become.

For instance, there is no doubt the individuals (in this case, players) who brazenly boast about their success and take complete credit possess great talent, but they should also be aware and acknowledge the fact that their success is often a result of a collective team effort, or, sometimes, even a matter of luck. Suppose, a person of high stature and relevant influence sees a player perform at the right time, they can easily draft that player into a team. So, here, the player should be humble enough to acknowledge that apart from his talent, this chance encounter with the influential person led to their selection in the team. Also, not to forget the training the player may be receiving from their coach and the support they may be getting from their family.

At times, when the players taste success in the early stages of their career, they tend to display youthful bravado and impudence. These traits, when left unchecked, can lead to misadventures and even downfall of their promising careers. So, it is important to be aware and acknowledge that no matter how smart or talented you are, your success is not yours alone to boast. There are circumstances and people who deserve the credit where it is due. This humility will take you a long way in your career.

Ajinkya Rahane is neither a superstar like Virat Kohli nor is he regarded as *"bindas"* (fearless) like Rohit Sharma. Yet, his humble nature is quite endearing. He is one of the rare players in modern cricket who is quintessentially modest. Let's go back to that infamous 2021 Adelaide Test: the team gets humiliated in the first match of the series (36 all out in the second innings), and then their captain Virat Kohli had to leave the match mid-way to attend the birth of his first child. Enter Ajinkya Rahane, the stand-in captain, who plays an incredible knock at the iconic Melbourne Cricket Ground, leading his team to victory in the second Test. Eventually, India wins the series by a margin of 2-1, despite losing many of its key players during the series. For someone who led India to one of their greatest-ever series wins, Rahane was at his modest best when he was asked to sum up his role in the victory, saying he only looked good as a leader because everyone else contributed.

Rahane, in his post-match press conference, showed no airs and graces about India's monumental Test win under his captaincy. Until then, India had only won a solitary Test series in Australia in nearly 70 years, and here was a man who wasn't even a regular captain, taking on the toughest assignment in Test cricket—and didn't bother to go over the top in his celebration.

"It's an honour to lead the country. It [the win] was not about me but about the team. I looked good because everyone contributed. For us, it was about having that character on the field, having that fighting spirit, the right attitude," said Rahane in the post-match presser when asked about his captaincy stint. Only a humble player like Ajinkya Rahane could have underplayed his role in such a historic win in his inimitable style. That's such a great learning for any youngster regardless of the field they are working in.

It is no secret that generally humble people are liked and admired by others, and they often become role models for those around them. When it comes to endearing humility, who can forget Rahul Dravid? Despite all his achievements, he still behaves the same with everyone he meets. So much so that when Virat Kohli got a special cap from Dravid before his 100th Test match, he recalled his first meeting with the head coach. "I couldn't have received it from a better person (Dravid), one of my childhood heroes. I still have the picture in my house from my U-15 NCA days, when I was looking at you while getting a picture with you! Today, I get my 100th Test cap from you, so indeed it has been a great journey and one that continues to grow hopefully," Kohli recalled warmly while sharing the said picture. It was the endearing humility of Dravid that made a lasting impression, not only for Kohli but everyone who come across the legend.

Wicketkeeper-batsman Sanju Samson, in one of his interview with Vimal Kumar in November 2024 at his home in Thiruvananthapuram, mentioned what is unique about Dravid is that he speaks to the groundsmen the same way he speaks to the team owners. Always respectful, always willing to take an opinion from others and eager to learn, Dravid embodies one of the key traits of humble people. They know they may be good, but they are not perfect. No matter how successful they become, they never put on airs and are always open to listening, learning, and improving themselves. This ability to look for information and knowledge no matter its source and implementing these learnings in enhancing their skills form the backbone of their humility.

Let me (Vimal Kumar) share a personal anecdote about MS Dhoni and how I was touched by his humble nature. It was the launch event of my first book *Sachin: Cricketer of the Century*. In 2013, Dhoni was at the peak of his career, having won the 2011 World Cup. When I approached him to speak on behalf of Sachin Tendulkar, he readily agreed. On March 20, 2013, at Delhi's Taj Hotel, I greeted Tendulkar and momentarily 'forgot' that Dhoni was around, as I was so overwhelmed by the magnetic presence of the "God of Cricket." Dhoni, an equally great cricketer unaccustomed to such occurrences where he is left alone and waiting, could have been easily hurt and could have expressed his displeasure. Instead, Dhoni understood the occasion so well and said: *"Aaj toh tum mujhe bhool sakte ho, banta hai.* (Today, you can afford to forget me. It's understandable)." He also implied that he understands that such things happen when a legend like Sachin Tendulkar is around. This story is more than a decade old, but every time I think of this incident, it gives me goosebumps and remains my abiding memory of Dhoni's humility.

Being humble also means being open to others' ideas and suggestions and pay appropriate attention to everyone you meet. You truly listen to others without any pretence. You care for the person in front of you and know that everyone around you can help you become better. The staggering success of MS Dhoni and Rohit Sharma in the history of IPL has a lot to do with their humble nature. Both have led their teams to the IPL finals several times, yet they maintain a humble demeanour sans grandiosity. You will be tired of listening to countless stories from their teammates on how these two leaders, with their humble attitude, made the dressing room feel like home, keeping the team motivated throughout the long duration of the tournament.

Life is constantly changing. Sometimes, you are the star, and other times, you feel that world around you is crumbling. Your humility keeps you rooted to the ground. The word "humility" word comes from "humus", which means "earth". It is quite natural for a lot of us to be arrogant when we taste success, and in that state of mind, we tend to say or do things which hurt others, leading to strained relationships. At the time, we may not realize the impact of our words and actions, but as time passes, we start to realize what we should have done differently and wish that we had remained humble.

Being humble brings numerous benefits to people who practice it. First, it allows you to connect with people on a deeper level. People open up to you and begin to trust you. You demonstrate gratitude, which fills you with positivity, and this positivity attracts others to support your success. After every win, Dhoni always encouraged the youngest member to hold the trophy while placing himself in a far corner of the team photo. Such small acts of generosity have a profound impact on younger players, who feel that they have contributed to the victory. This reflects the attitude and mindset of a secure leader who knows that success is for everyone to cherish and always a result of team effort. This secure mindset also allows the leader to act selflessly.

In the 2023 IPL season, MS Dhoni invariably batted at number 7 or 8, and often faced just two to four balls in an inning. Despite being a great batsman himself, Dhoni knew that his best days as a batter were behind him, and he always promoted more deserving batters for the opening order. He never really had an enormous ego. In sporting world, especially among elite athletes, acknowledging that you are no longer at your peak and publicly demonstrating it through your actions is never easy. This is simply impossible if one is not humble.

Another benefit of humility is that it helps you develop strong emotional wellness, self-regulation, and resilience. Even in victory, a humble person will seek to learn rather than indulge in self-praise. They learn from their mistakes and work on it without worrying about others' opinions. A humble person keeps their ego in check because they are aware that if their ego takes over, then others may withhold honest opinions, suggestions, and advice, and this can hurt them and their team in the long run. On the other hand, if you are someone who frequently displays your ego and aggression, chances are that you will surround yourself by those who may seem nice at first, but will undermine you the moment they get an opportunity.

How Do You Develop Humility?

One of the easiest ways to do this is to reflect on your life with all humanness. When Shikhar Dhawan, one of the India's finest ODI openers, was interviewed in 2023 about his comeback in the team, his candour bowled everyone over. It was rarest of the rare occurrences in Indian cricket where a teammate, a direct competitor to a younger player, was brutally honest. This stems from humanness. Let me tell you the backstory.

Dhawan had long been renowned for his impressive records in ICC tournaments. However, his dwindling form over the last few years, amid the rise of young talent, saw him lose his place in the Indian team. Dhawan last played in December 2022, and he was out of the reckoning for a place in the 2023 ICC Cricket World Cup (ODI) team. However, when asked directly whether he would have picked himself over Shubman Gill—who eventually replaced him—Dhawan's response left the reporter astounded. In an interview with *Aaj Tak* TV, Dhawan was asked if he were the selector of the team or the captain, would he have given himself more chances? Dhawan nonchalantly responded about Gill: "I feel the way Shubman is playing at the moment... Like he was playing two formats and performing well in Tests and T20s. He has been playing more matches in the international circuit, and I wasn't." When the reporter clarified whether Dhawan would have picked Gill over himself, the Delhi batsman simply replied "Yes," leaving not only the journalist but also cricket fans worldwide amazed at the remark.

When thinking about humility, we must remember one essential fact: the two most important events in your life—your birth and your death—are not in your hands. So, if you cannot control these, how can you be certain of controlling other events of your life? It's just an illusion that you are in control. This understanding brings you closer to the truth of life and makes you humble. Reflect on some of the greatest people and observe how they are remembered—the legacy they left behind and the love they received from those who knew them.

Practicing gratitude is another route to attaining a humble demeanour. When you are grateful, you are aware of how privileged you're as compared to others. There was something beyond your control (like being born into a rich family, having associations with influential people, or inheriting generational wealth, business, or influence) which allowed you access to the opportunities which others could not, despite being in similar career stages. However, the awareness that you don't deserve all the accolades for yourself allows you to see others' contributions in your life. You then tend to be grateful of and acknowledge the privilege you have. This, in turn, makes you humble.

A third way to cultivate humility is by nurturing an unsatiable curiosity to learn and grow. When you are excited about learning, you do not worry about by whom or where the lesson comes from. It could come from a young person or from a setback. Whatever the source, you must develop this mindset of being open to learn. This is what fosters humility.

Sometimes, dark realities of life make you humble. Sometimes, it's a particular sport. We can look at sports as a reflection of life—there is birth, learning, failure, aspiration, success, and defeat. You will see your life experiences reflected in sports. The way cricket is a great leveller, life, too, is one. Your experiences teach you a lot.

Cricket players with humility often show these behaviours:

1. **Being a good sport:** On the field, there can be fierce rivalry between players, but at the end of the day, you respect your opponents. You play by the rules of the game and do not get carried away by success. Ultimately, it is a team sport where everyone has played a role.

2. **Accept defeat and congratulate the winners:** In sports, and in life, you cannot win all the time. Every game starts afresh, and the outcome of the game depends on many factors. That's the beauty of the game. Sometimes you win, sometimes you lose. Humble people accept defeat wholeheartedly and look for ways to bounce back stronger because of the lessons they learn. (For instance, India was out of 2007 ICC Cricket World Cup and the morale of the team was down, but then the team bounced back stronger to win their first 2007 ICC World Twenty20 Cup in that same year and the next edition of Cricket World Cup (ODI) in 2011.)

3. **Celebrate others' success:** By appreciating someone else's achievement for the way they played and examples they set, you are demonstrating your humility. This way, you convey it to the word that you appreciate and acknowledge something which you might not have. Accepting that someone else can be better than you does not make you any less; it allows you to develop humility.

4. **Learning from mistakes:** Great players with humility can learn from anyone. It's not about ego, but about being open to suggestions and ideas, regardless of the source it comes from. In the end, you want to improve and do whatever it takes to make yourself a better person. In that context, someone who is open to learning and improving themselves will demonstrate and practice tremendous humility in all aspects of life.

Humility is a trait which will never go out of fashion. We all understand that our personal talent can only take us so far. What will matter in the long run is how we took people along and made them feel in our company. For that to happen in a positive way, you need a great deal of humility because humility is the glue which binds people in a relationship. This allows them to trust each other at the highest level, which is essential for a fulfilling life.

BUILDING AND MANAGING A TEAM

11

Vision

Ability to See What Doesn't Exist, and Make It Happen

"THE ONLY THING WORSE THAN BEING BLIND IS HAVING SIGHT AND NO VISION."

—HELEN KELLER, American author, disability rights advocate, political activist

Vision is your ability to create things that do not yet exist and to show determination in making them a reality. It's your mental picture of tomorrow that directs your actions today. What separates leaders from others is their ability to see things which are not seen by most people. While ordinary people are responsible for making today better, leaders are known to creating a better tomorrow based on their vision.

While the entire cricketing world was content with five-day Test matches, there was one visionary who thought cricket could be improved with some much-needed innovation. Although it wasn't an easy road for Kerry Packer—an Australian media tycoon—to fight the mighty cricket board of his time, the confidence that he had in his vision made him relentlessly pursue his mission. Despite facing court battles, Packer launched a rebel World Series Cricket (a commercial professional cricket competition) in 1976 which featured world's top 35 players.

The self-styled "Super Tests", with teams like Australian XI, Rest of the World XI, and the West Indies revolutionized the sports as floodlight and coloured clothing in cricket were used for the first time. Super Tests were a series of unofficial Test matches played in 1977 and 1978 as a part of World Series Cricket. When Kerry Packer passed away in 2005, the great Shane Warne eulogized him succinctly: "Everyone in the world of cricket owes (Packer) so much." Former International Cricket Council (ICC) President Ehsan Mani noted, "Very few people in the history of the game, either players or administrators, can be said to have changed the game, but Kerry Packer can rightly be considered as someone who did just that."

Three decades later, Lalit Modi, Indian businessman and former cricket administrator, did the same by introducing the Indian Premier League (IPL). The heady cocktail of Bollywood and cricket was ridiculed in the beginning, and very few imagined that the blitzkrieg T20 format would transform the game forever. Though T20 revolution initially began in England in 2005, it is the IPL that paved the way for hundreds of private T20 leagues around the world.

Both these examples exhibit a similar pattern: everything was going fine, and it wouldn't have made any difference to

VISIONARIES ARE LEADERS WHO CAN PEEP INTO THE FUTURE AND DEFINE HOW THE WORLD SHOULD LOOK

the existing set-up if these innovations were not introduced. But then you had visionaries who were not satisfied with the status quo and were keen to disrupt it by bringing in new perspectives, markets, and value to the table. Visionaries are leaders who can peep into the future and define how the world should look. Once they create a mental model, they work tirelessly to transform their vision into a reality.

Why Do You Need a Vision When Everything Is Going Fine?

In his illustrious career, Mahendra Singh Dhoni has had many triumphs under his leadership. Yet the 2023 IPL trophy will always be particularly special to him because it came under enormously challenging circumstances. Dhoni was no longer the player he used to be, but he never gave up. He demoted himself in the batting order and persuaded Ravindra Jadeja to forget any misunderstanding he had with the Chennai Super Kings. Ultimately, it was Jadeja's winning shot that turned the tables on the Gujarat Titans in the final.

In a conversation with Jadeja during World Test Championship in London, Jadeja mentioned it to me (Vimal Kumar) that it was his dedication to Dhoni that fuelled his determination. He also revealed how Dhoni not only has a solid vision for the franchise but also for individual players and their growth. This is what motivates young players like Ruturaj Gaikwad and veterans like Ajinkya Rahane and Ravindra Jadeja to give their best.

Having a vision ensures that you have clarity. You are not perturbed by the failures you face along the way because you know that they are a part of the journey towards the larger goal you have in front of you. In almost every IPL, Chennai Super Kings are derided for their player choices during auctions, but sooner or later, everything falls in place. Critics are often forced to eat humble pie, largely due to the vision of one man—MS Dhoni. Having a vision also gives clarity on expectations

YOU CAN HAVE A VISION, BUT IF YOU DON'T HAVE A TEAM TO WORK ON THAT VISION, THEN IT NEVER BECOMES A REALITY

you have from each member of your team. You can have a vision, but if you don't have a team to work on that vision, then it never becomes a reality. A visionary leader clearly defines the exact roles and goals for each team member in achieving the vision they set for them and ensures that they give their best, increasing the likelihood of success.

Why Do People Get Inspired?

If your vision is compelling and aspirational, people will naturally be attracted to it. Once they commit to your vision, they gain meaning and purpose in what they do on a day-to-day basis. It is the power of vision that brings out extreme efforts from seemingly ordinary people. We all are aware that we are powerful, but that power only translates into action when it is directed towards a vision.

While there are leaders who have a vision to disrupt things even when things are going fine, some visionaries create that disruption out of extreme dissatisfaction with the current state. They are not happy with what they have and they know that they have the power and ability to change it. Failures they experienced in past fuel the desire to weave a vision for the future. You can see, for instance, how English cricket has transformed in recent years in every format. Former captain Eoin Morgan changed the template for white-ball cricket; this was taken to another level by Ben Stokes and coach Brendon McCullum in Test cricket. As a result, Team England, today, not only holds both the ODI and T20 World Cup titles but is also considered one of the top teams in Test cricket.

The process of crafting a vision has basically got three elements: discovery, dissemination, and implementation. First stage is about discovering a vision, followed by disseminating that vision to the people who will help you achieve it, and then implementing the plan or acting on that vision. All these elements are crucial, but the most important part is the actual discovery of your mission. This requires the leaders to craft a mission that is not only aspirational but also practical. It should generate such an excitement in stakeholders that they are inspired to stretch their limits and bring out their best. Even when difficulties arise and confusion prevails, a vision is the compass that guides them to the right path.

Disseminating your vision requires conveying it in such a way that it truly becomes a shared goal and is not dependent on one person. Because if it is dependent on one person, then it cannot be sustained in the long term. In an environment where a vision is shared and everyone on the team is clear on their goals, the entire team works as a well-oiled machinery to make that vision a reality.

While having a vision is important, it is not everyone's cup of tea, and there are reasons for that. First, many people are comfortable with the status quo. People seldom want to change if things are going fine. Most of us are so well-adjusted to our current reality that we are reluctant to change unless we are forced to. It is here the rare talent of a visionary leader—who sees a different and better future even when things are going fine—comes in and changes the game. Second, vision requires consistency. Most of us start things enthusiastically but struggle to keep up with the necessary efforts over a long period of time.

How Can One Develop a Visionary Mindset?

Visionaries can see the things that do not exist at the moment and imagine future possibilities. To build this quality, you need to do three things:

1. **Challenge the status quo:** Train your mind to not settle into a comfort zone. You should constantly think about the ways in which things or situations could be improved. Imagine what was never imagined before.

2. **Have immense courage:** Muster the courage to do things that have never been done before, and that can make others uncomfortable. You may face resistance and people may think that you are impractical. Despite this resistance at first, you should be able to summon the courage to swim against the tide and achieve what you have set out to.

3. **Cultivate emotional intelligence:** You can be a dreamer, but the dreams can come true with the help of of your teammates. How you identify talent, place people in the right roles, and create a sense of purpose and mission will define whether your vision can become a reality or not. There's an African proverb which says: If you want to go fast, go alone. If you want to go far, then you need to walk with others.

Vision is one of the most important elements of success. A compelling vision unites everyone towards a goal and inspires them to give their best in everything they do. They are ready to undergo pain and bring out their resilience to ensure their success. If successfully crafted and implemented, a great vision always leaves a legacy behind and becomes a source of inspiration for future generations. After all, people always remember those who can see what others can not, and more importantly, are thrilled to learn and understand how that vision can be turned into a reality.

12

Judgment

Making the Right Decisions by Weighing Pros and Cons

"GOOD JUDGMENT IS THE RESULT OF EXPERIENCE AND EXPERIENCE IS THE RESULT OF BAD JUDGMENT."

—MARK TWAIN, American writer and humourist

During the Indian cricket team's tour of the West Indies in 2023, India's captain Rohit Sharma had a difficult decision to make: which teammate should he partner with as an opening batsman in Test cricket? There was the temptation to stick with Shubman Gill who had opened with him in the previous Test (at the Oval in London) and on other occasions in the past. Or, should he pick 26-year-old Ruturaj Gaikwad who was among the front-runners? However, Rohit Sharma decided to go with the younger (21-year-old) southpaw Yashasvi Jaiswal. The Indian captain's judgment (or hunch) was based on what he saw in Jaiswal during a net practice session leading up to the first game, which I (Vimal Kumar) was lucky to witness from close quarters in the Caribbean. Jaiswal not only scored a terrific hundred (171) on debut in Dominica, but more significantly, he went on to play a decisive role in India beating England six months later.

In that series, England's "Bazball" approach was supposed to conquer India (again after a decade or so), and it seemed increasingly possible when senior players like Virat Kohli and KL Rahul were absent from the series. Yashasvi Jaiswal defied his age and experience and went on to score nearly 700 runs in the five-match series—far more than the combined total of the next two batsmen in the series.

"I have spoken a lot about him in Vizag as well; people outside the dressing room have also talked about him. I do not want to talk too much about him now. He has started his career on a high, and I want him to continue doing so. Yeah, he looks like a good player," Sharma, his captain, said after repeated queries by the media on the young cricketer. It was not that the skipper did not want to praise his young players publicly, he just understood that too much praise from a captain can be counter-productive as well, so he avoided it. Having gone through similar phases in his own career, Rohit Sharma was aware of the pitfalls when the media gets carried away by a sensational display from an emerging talent.

Leaders are leaders because they can see what others cannot. Not only can they see which is beyond others' sight, but they also take action, which allows them to realize that vision. With relevant data, information, and analysis in front of them, they are

LEADERS ARE LEADERS BECAUSE THEY CAN SEE WHAT OTHERS CANNOT

required to make decisions, and this ability to decide—even when the future remains hazy (despite all the data, information, and analysis)—is called judgment. A leader needs many competencies to be successful, but having a good judgment becomes the defining quality of a leader. One wrong move, and you may be out of business. Nokia, once the leading mobile manufacturer, seemed inimitable. Everyone felt that no one stood a chance in front of Nokia. However, one wrong judgment—choosing Symbian over Android operating system—changed the game for them. That is why judgment, as a leadership quality, is always rated highly.

Judgment—the ability to combine personal qualities with relevant knowledge and experience to form opinions and make decisions—is "the core of exemplary leadership" according to Noel Tichy and Warren Bennis, authors of *Judgment: How Winning Leaders Make Great Calls*. Not everyone is born with the ability to make sound judgments, but it is a quality that can be learned if we closely observe how we react, learn, and make decisions.

The first step in developing a good judgment is understanding our emotional status while making a decision. Are we excited, fearful, or indifferent? What are we feeling? Why are we feeling the way we are feeling? These questions are about our mental state. In sports and in life, emotional stability determines the accuracy of your judgment.

THE FIRST STEP IN DEVELOPING A GOOD JUDGMENT IS UNDERSTANDING OUR EMOTIONAL STATUS WHILE MAKING A DECISION

Please excuse us for digressing a little, but we would like to share an interesting (but relevant) non-cricket story with you all. In 1983, during the Cold War (between the United States and the Soviet Union), when Lieutenant Colonel Stanislav Petrov, duty officer at Soviet Air Defence Forces' Oko (nuclear early-warning system command center), received a message regarding a missile attack on USSR from the United States through its machines, he did not panic. He judiciously thought it through and decided not to alert anyone based on his suspicion that it was unlikely for the attack to take place at that time and manner in which it was reported. Later, they found out that it was indeed a false alarm; apparently the reflection of sunrays got the machines confused. Mr. Petrov could make that good judgment call because he could think logically even in that moment of great stress. This good judgment prevented a retaliatory nuclear attack by the USSR that could have led to a full-scale nuclear war. This ability to keep our emotions in check in stressful situations and make sound and informed decisions is what distinguishes people with good judgment from those with poor judgment.

The second element of building good judgment is how you learn. It is about how you learn from the people around you and from the written word. People with good judgment give their undivided attention to those they are with. They are observant and learn to understand non-verbal cues. They can sense and understand more deeply, and ask probing questions that yield insights—crucial traits lacking in those who listen merely for the sake of it. Now, let's return to Rohit Sharma and Yashasvi Jaiswal's story.

"Do not be in awe of any player. Whether it is me, your captain, or senior players, or coach, or your opponents. Do not get overwhelmed by the highest cricket platform which is Test cricket. Never ever think that someone has done you a favour by bringing you here today. You have come a long way in such a short time, and it is because of your ability and confidence," the Indian captain was heard telling Jaiswal on the eve of his debut. The southpaw (Jaiswal) averaged 80 in first-class cricket, scored 9 centuries in 15 Ranji Trophy matches, and had a phenomenal run in the 2023 IPL season, which brought him in the limelight. When Jaiswal became the hero of the series in March 2023 against England, everyone was singing his praises, except his captain. Because Rohit Sharma had done his part behind the camera.

"You are the boss or the king when you are facing a bowler. No one will guide you on the pitch; you are on your own. But this isn't something new for you or any other cricketer. We all are on our own when we face a bowler. The only thing which helps us is our focus and concentration, and the belief that what has worked for me so far will continue to take me forward. Your friends and teammates and well-wishers will give you a lot of advice and suggestions, while all may be well-intended, you should be able to decide for yourself what you must implement and what to leave for the future. It is a journey of continued learning," said the Indian captain to Jaiswal[1], who was nodding and listening like a keen student.

Another aspect of learning is how they read. They don't simply read—they read critically. Unlike in conversations, where body

---

[1] Kumar, Vimal. "MC Exclusive I Don't Be in Awe of Any Player: Captain Rohit Sharma's Special Motivational Class for Yashasvi Jaiswal." Moneycontrol, July 12, 2023. https://www.moneycontrol.com/news/trends/sports/mc-exclusive-i-dont-be-in-awe-of-any-player-captain-rohit-sharmas-special-motivational-class-for-yashasvi-jaiswal-10948071.html.

language or the tone of the voice offers non-verbal cues, everything they read needs to be taken with a pinch of salt. They are also adept in understanding what to read and what not. Sometimes, information overload blurs the decision-making abilities of several leaders.

SOMETIMES, INFORMATION OVERLOAD BLURS THE DECISION-MAKING ABILITIES OF SEVERAL LEADERS

The type of people you surround yourself with, too, has an immense impact on your judgment. When Chinese business magnate and investor, Jack Ma, was building his empire, he knew that technology wasn't his strong suit, so, he hired John Wu from Yahoo to provide an edge. Both were unique people with different skillsets, but they complimented each other. By observing Wu at work, Jack Ma could understand and learn from a different perspective. To have good judgment, one needs to be surrounded with people who tell them what they need to hear, not what they want to. This diversity hugely helps the leaders to cultivate better judgment.

A lot of spicy and imaginative stories were doing rounds when Rohit Sharma took over the captaincy from Virat Kohli. Rumours were rife that they both do not get along well. However, Sharma has always had immense respect for Kohli, who, in his inimitable style, had led India gloriously for several years. I spoke to several members of the Indian team who confirmed that Sharma would often consult Kohli for advice. While he doesn't always listen and implement all of Kohli's suggestions (as a leader must eventually make their own judgments and be responsible for them), valuing Kohli's opinions and showing respect for his experience as a senior leader and predecessor helps maintain a good and positive team culture.

Learning also comes from experience. Being part of a larger team and being with them as a team member does teach valuable lessons. Instead of having this attitude that they know everything, great leaders are always ready to get their hands dirty on the ground. These experiences help them a lot when they are put in a similar situation; it helps them make better decisions in comparison to those who have not faced such situations in the past. Serial entrepreneurs exemplify this—learning from each of their venture and applying those learnings to make better judgment calls in future. That's why company boardrooms are filled with experienced individuals who can guide the leader of the firm to navigate cautiously through unfamiliar situations. Their advice helps develop the judgment of the leader immensely.

This practice is evident in the operations of IPL's most successful team—Mumbai Indians (MI). From the inception of the franchise, MI has been surrounded by strong leaders from various countries and different profile. The contrasting opinions are rigorously discussed, and once a consensus is reached, the team moves ahead in that one direction. This collaboration is one of the reasons of MI's great legacy in IPL history.

Finally, judgment is also about one's ability to take risks while making decisions and being ready to face the consequences. There will always be an element of doubt in whatever decisions you take as a leader, but if you are prepared to bear the consequences and correct your course before it's late, it is still manageable. The problem with a lot of leaders is that they get entangled with different psychological biases without realizing it. For instance, you invest in a stock thinking that it is going to give you good returns. Initially, it did give you returns, but of late, its prices are going down. Instead of pulling out your investment, you continue investing money in it. There are two biases in play here: first, endowment bias (you do not want to part with something you own), and second, sunk cost bias (if you have already invested heavily in this stock, you tend to put a little more lest it turns around and gives you a good return). Like these, there are many other biases, and as a leader we need to be very careful about going through the same when making decisions.

In sports and in life, judgment of a person plays a crucial role in the final outcome. Following your passion without judgment can make you do things you may not be proud of retrospectively. Focus without judgment can take you down the wrong path, and success without proper judgment may not be sustainable. So, in all analysis, judgment plays one of the most significant roles when it comes to shaping the life of a successful leader. If Yashasvi Jaiswal goes on to become a great player in the coming decade, some of the credit will go to Rohit Sharma's judgment made in Caribbean in 2023.

13

Perseverance

The More You Deter Me, the More Determined I Become

"MANY OF LIFE'S FAILURES ARE PEOPLE WHO DID NOT REALIZE HOW CLOSE THEY WERE TO SUCCESS WHEN THEY GAVE UP."

—THOMAS EDISON, American inventor and businessman

There's this one fascinating story from the 1990s that exemplifies the trait of perseverance. Harsha Bhogle, India's most renowned cricket commentator, often shares this story of the former Sri Lankan batter Marvan Atapattu to highlight the power of perseverance. In his Test debut for Sri Lanka, Atapattu scored consecutive ducks in two innings, leading to his immediate exclusion from the team. Undeterred, he went back to domestic cricket, training harder and scoring well. After 21 months, he got another chance, but managed only 0 and 1, and was once again dropped from the team. Still, he refused to give up and continued to work relentlessly for another opportunity. When a third opportunity came knocking, again he had to leave the cricket pitch with two more ducks. But, instead of quitting, he kept grinding for years. Despite repeated failures, Atapattu eventually broke through.

Six years after his debut, he scored runs consistently and went on to accumulate over 5,000 runs for Sri Lanka, including 16 centuries and 6 double hundreds. In his international career, he scored over 14,000 runs for the team over 16 years. Not only did he conquer his early struggles but he also went on to captain his country. His story is a powerful reminder that success doesn't come easy and is often preceded by numerous setbacks.

Perseverance means not giving up despite rejections, obstacles, and not being able to see the proverbial light at the end of the tunnel. Bhogle loves to share Atapattu's story as a lesson that, in cricket and in life, perseverance in the face of rejection and failure can lead to extraordinary achievements.

So, How to Develop Perseverance?

Building new habits is tough, especially for someone who has been wired in a certain way. It's no wonder why most of the New Year's resolutions are broken within the first month. The thinking brain wants you to live in the present—enjoy that chocolate, take that nap, and be happy with life's small pleasures—instead of doing things which may have a long-term benefit but require short-term sacrifices. It's hardly surprising why most of us give up.

Those who do not give up are determined souls. They know where they are heading and what they are doing. For them, it's not about looking at repeated failures as the final straw, but a step towards being ready for greater success. Difficulties in life prepare them to stick to the path they choose because they know it is the right one.

Now, let me (Vimal Kumar) give you a personal account with the Indian middle-order batter Sarfaraz Khan and his father Naushad Khan.

"Vimal sir, mark my words today. One day, my son will play for India and you will interview him," prophesied Naushad Khan in front of Mumbai's iconic Wankhede Stadium on the eve of Indian team's World Cup final game against Sri Lanka in 2011. As a television reporter with *CNN-IBN*, I was interviewing some of the local coaches in Mumbai just to gauge the mood of the World Cup final fever. Once the interview was over, Naushad introduced me to his then 13-year-old son, Sarfaraz. I do not recall the exact conversation with the young boy, but much was being said about him in Mumbai's cricketing circles as he had already broken the record for the highest score in the Harris Shield inter-school tournament, making 439 for Rizvi Springfield in an innings that featured 56 fours and 12 sixes, a few months ago. Sarfaraz Khan was being seen as the next big thing from the famous Mumbai school of batting.

A couple of years later, Sarfaraz was a part of the India squad for the Under-19 Cricket World Cup in UAE in 2014. Having scored 211 runs in six games at an average of 70.33, Sarfaraz was all set for his graduation to the next level. In the very next year, (in 2015,) Royal Challengers Bangalore bought him for ₹50 lakh, and he soon became the youngest player to play in the IPL. He was cynosure of all eyes for his unbeaten knock of 45 runs off just 21 balls against Rajasthan Royals, so much so that the then RCB skipper Virat Kohli bowed in front of the 17-year-old—a fitting acknowledgment of his talent.

The rising graph of his career continued with him finishing as the second-highest run-scorer in the Under-19 World Cup in Bangladesh, (355 runs in 6 matches). By this time, not only his father Naushad but also a lot of former cricketers started talking about his next big break—making it to the senior Indian team. An enviable CV of 566 runs at an excellent average of 70.75 across the two Under-19 Cricket World Cups, it seemed only a matter of time. In the meantime, Sarfaraz had made his first-class debut in 2014 as well.

And suddenly, his journey took a mysterious turn. He came under scrutiny for his age-related controversy, his on-field fights, and disputes with players, umpires, and even with selectors did not help his case. Eventually, he left Mumbai and joined Uttar Pradesh's Ranji team. It seemed that another talented player had lost his way. However, the element of perseverance ran in his blood. Soon, he made a comeback in 2019-20 season for Mumbai. His appetite to score big runs returned. While he kept piling up runs in first-class cricket, Sarfaraz's sustained struggle in the most important tournament of IPL was baffling. From being retained for ₹4 crore by RCB in 2018, Sarfaraz narrowly avoided the ignominy of being forgotten when Delhi Capitals picked him up for his base price of ₹20 lakh in the 2023 IPL auction.

Yet, the desire to play Test cricket—the greatest challenge

and ultimate ambition for any cricketer—never faded for Sarfaraz. And as the saying goes, the harder one tries, the luckier one gets. In 2024, against England, Sarfaraz finally made it to the India squad and soon debuted in the five-match Test series. This, of course, had a lot to with the absence of Virat Kohli and KL Rahul in that series, but more importantly, it was Sarfaraz's perseverance that made him believe that he would get an opportunity to play for India sooner or later. That unshakable self-belief made him endure the frustrating years of waiting.

"I felt a burden lift off me. Whatever hard work my father has done for me, I've not let it go to waste," said Sarfaraz after his first match in Rajkot. "My father had this dream of playing for India, but our situation at home at that time was not strong enough to support him. Then he decided to work hard on his kids. So, he worked hard on me, and now he is working on my brother [Musheer] as well," added Sarfaraz in his first-ever press conference as an India player.

The prophecy of his father and his dream came true. It was only possible because of his father's perseverance as much as his son's. Just imagine if Sarfaraz had left cricket after seeing his Under-19 World Cup teammates like Shreyas Iyer, Sanju Samson, Kuldeep Yadav, Ishan Kishan, Rishabh Pant, and Washington Sundar all debuting years before him and establishing themselves as accomplished players. To end this story, I did get a call from Naushad Khan who joyously said, *"Aapko kaha tha na Vimal sir, aapko yaad hai na??"* (I had told you, Vimal sir. I hope you remember that.)

That's the story of perseverance. Backing your own conviction unflinchingly.

One of the questions that often arises is whether perseverance is a gift from God to a select few or a skill that can be developed by anyone. Angela Duckworth, who has studied grit and resilience, believes that perseverance is a skill which can be mastered by anyone with the right mindset and perspective on life. There are four ingredients for building perseverance, and each can be gradually acquired and nurtured.

1. **Passion:** If you love what you do and get to do it every day, you are lucky. There are a very few people who are aware of their passion, and even fewer have the opportunity to pursue it every day. Once you observe yourself and notice the areas you are interested in, be curious. Experiment with new things and see if it gives you happiness. Try to develop the areas that give you immense pleasure and where learning comes quickly. These are the traces of your passion, and you need to nurture them. From an early age, Sarfaraz knew he loved cricket. His father helped him discover his passion, but the talent was already there. Slowly and steadily, Sarfaraz built his passion for the game. Passion is the first ingredient which opens the door to perseverance.

2. **Practice:** Merely having passion is not enough. Many people dream of success and aspire to make a name for themselves. There are only a few, however, who are committed to practice consistently towards their goals. While people notice the success and adulation, they often overlook the hard work put in by those successful people. Take the story of Deepika Mhatre, who demanding life, of working as a housemaid in five houses across Mumbai to support her family. Yet deep down she knew she was a performer. When the opportunity knocked on her door in the form of a stand-up comedy session arranged by her employers for local housemaids, she grabbed it with both

hands. She practiced diligently and her performance was noticed by one and all. From there on, she did not look back and continued developing her art, reaching a position where she could not only enjoy doing what she loved but also make a career out of it.

3. **Purpose:** Another ingredient in building perseverance is having a strong purpose. Once there is clarity on what the person wants to achieve, not just for themselves but for the benefit of others around them, they are ready to persevere. When Dadarao Bilhore's 16-year-old son Prakash was crushed under a vehicle due to a pothole, Bilhore's purpose in life changed. He took a vow to fill as many as potholes he could so no other person would meet the same fate as his son. It was a difficult task and laden with challenges, but he managed to continue his mission. As of the last count, he had filled more than 600 potholes and is determined to do more until his last breath.

4. **Hope:** Hope is the fourth and final ingredient for developing perseverance. Hope is the belief that our efforts matter, and sooner or later, we will get the results we are striving for. The beginning may be small, but small steps are the foundation of bigger things. Hope is something which keeps people going despite the rejections and disappointments they face.

No wonder, when Angela Duckworth[1] studied successful people and the reasons for their success, she could prove that in

---

[1] DR, Duckworth AL; Peterson C; Matthews MD; Kelly. "Grit: Perseverance and Passion for Long-Term Goals." Journal of Personality and Social Psychology. Accessed October 28, 2024. https://pubmed.ncbi.nlm.nih.gov/17547490/.

the end, it is not just the talent that makes one successful but one's ability to have the courage to continue despite obstacles which makes a difference. One quality which we need to instill in our younger generation, if they want to be successful, is grit. Because there are many who are talented, but there are only a few who can continue despite obstacles, and that is the only thing which matters between success and failure.

14

Teamwork

Together We Can Go Far, Achieve Anything

"THE STRENGTH OF THE TEAM IS EACH INDIVIDUAL MEMBER. THE STRENGTH OF EACH MEMBER IS THE TEAM."

—PHIL JACKSON, former American basketball player and coach

Since 2013, the Indian Test cricket team had been unbeaten on its home turf, securing a record 16 series victories under the combined leadership of MS Dhoni, Virat Kohli, and Rohit Sharma. In January 2023, the English cricket team arrived in India with an ambition of emulating their last victorious tour (led by Alastair Cook), when they became the last visiting team to defeat India at home, a feat often considered the final frontier in cricketing challenges.

The English cricket team, led by the inspirational captain Ben Stokes and an outstanding coach Brendon McCullum, has been playing Test cricket in such an incredibly amazing way that a new term, 'Bazball', was coined to describe their aggressive methods. 'Bazball' nomenclature is derived from their coach McCullum's nickname (Baz). England's chances of winning were further boosted by the news that India's greatest modern-day batsman Virat Kohli was going to be absent from these highly anticipated contests in the five-match series. Along the way, India would also lose KL Rahul, who had performed outstandingly in South Africa prior to this series, and Ravindra Jadeja, another legend in the Indian team, too, would miss some matches due to fitness issues.

India started the series by losing the first Test in Hyderabad, a match they should have won. Captain Rohit Sharma faced severe criticism from all corners. As a premier and the most-experienced batsman in the team, he failed to score significantly in both innings. The notorious British media relentlessly pursued the Indian captain, and former players began questioning Sharma's 'relaxed' leadership style compared to the highly intense and aggressive brand of captaincy of his predecessor, Virat Kohli.

However, Rohit Sharma didn't lose sleep over it. Instead, he held a quiet meeting with his team members in the dressing room, sharing a simple message: "One defeat does not make us a bad team. We lost due to a once-in-a-lifetime performance from an individual (Ollie Pope's 196 runs). Let us try better, and we shall prevail." As it turned out, India made a staggering comeback, winning the next four matches emphatically. They became only the fourth team in nearly 150 years of Test cricket to win by a scoreline of 4-1 after losing the first match. And this happened after a gap of over 100 years. Notably, five debutants from India played in that series, and the highest run-scorer for India, Yashashvi Jaiswal, had played just four matches before. One of the most successful bowlers,

Kuldeep Yadav, had played just eight matches over seven years, and the critical innings of 90 runs in Ranchi was played by wicketkeeper Dhruv Jurel, who wouldn't have played at all if Rishabh Pant hadn't been injured, Ishan Kishan hadn't been absent, and KS Bharat hadn't lost his form midway.

"As the captain of this team, getting that result is very pleasing. I do not have enough words to describe this particular team that we have at this point. At different stages of the game, different Test matches, people put their hands up and got us through the line. It's a very proud moment, and I'm happy for the young boys who tasted success in Test cricket, which is very nice," captain Rohit Sharma explained to the host broadcaster after the series win in Dharamshala. What the captain meant that the strength of the team lay in each individual member, and the strength of each member lay in the team.

In simple terms, teamwork is collaborating with others to achieve a common goal. Everyone involved is focused on what is to be achieved and how their strengths can contribute to progress. It is true that the world only saw Neil Armstrong as the person who landed on the moon, but behind him were over 400,000 people who contributed, in various ways, to make that landing possible. There were scientists, engineers, technicians, researchers, and many other experts who did their jobs perfectly to ensure that Apollo 11 landed safely at its destination. The thrill of

IN SIMPLE TERMS, TEAMWORK IS COLLABORATING WITH OTHERS TO ACHIEVE A COMMON GOAL making something happen, even when you are not in the forefront, is the hallmark of a great team effort. Nothing in this world was achieved by a single person. You always require a team to back you, support you, and give you a push when you need it.

YOU ALWAYS REQUIRE A TEAM TO BACK YOU, SUPPORT YOU, AND GIVE YOU A PUSH WHEN YOU NEED IT

How Can One Form a Super-Productive Team That Delivers Consistently?

It all starts with a leader who has a strong vision. A visionary leader knows where they want to go and how they will reach there. This vision is the building block of the journey. All great teams know where they want to be and how they will get there. Someone at NASA dreamt of going to the moon, someone dreamt of flying, someone at Ford dreamt of creating cars that would defeat Ferrari at its own game, and so on. The vision of a person trying to achieve something significant is the cornerstone of creating a great team and instilling teamwork because it is this dream which drives everyone to put all their energies towards achieving it.

Kolkata has always been known for its love for cricket and other sports, in general. When the IPL initially began, Bollywood icon Shah Rukh Khan bought a cricket team and Sourav Ganguly was made its captain; a lot was expected from this franchise in the early years. However, from one controversy to another and repeated bad performances, the Kolkata Knight Riders (KKR) failed to make any mark in the first three seasons.

Forget about winning titles, KKR became the laughingstock of the IPL as they invariably finished at the bottom of the points table. Even one of the finest captains, Sourav Ganguly, along with cricket's greatest coach, John Buchanan, disastrously failed in forming a decent team, let alone a formidable one.

After the horrendously painful three seasons where they could not even qualify for the playoffs, SRK knew that his franchise needed a different approach. In 2011, KKR spent $2.4 million on Gautam Gambhir, who, though not a superstar like Virender Sehwag or Yuvraj Singh, was one of the architects of India's 2011 World Cup win. Underappreciated but deeply determined as a leader to prove himself, Gambhir led KKR to their maiden IPL playoffs (reaching the top four teams) that season. Although they didn't win the IPL title, it marked the beginning of a new journey. And, as they say, the rest is history. In the very next year, in 2012, KKR won their first IPL title by defeating MS Dhoni's Chennai Super Kings (CSK) at Chepauk, a feat akin to taming the tiger in its own den. Two seasons later, in 2014, KKR won another IPL trophy under Gambhir, making it clear that the first win wasn't just a fluke. From the perennial underachievers, KKR transformed into becoming tournament favourites in the years that followed.

Gautam Gambhir's departure in 2018 saw KKR struggle to maintain the same tempo each season. Over the next six seasons, SRK's franchise have had the World Cup-winning captains like Eoin Morgan to celebrated cricketers like Dinesh Karthik, Shreyas Iyer, and Nitish Rana at the helm. The coveted trophy, however, still eluded them. Such was Gambhir's impact as a leader that KKR brought him back in 2024 as a mentor, hoping for a turnaround. The reason for going back to Gambhir had also to do with his work as a successful mentor in the IPL with the Lucknow Super Giants who made it to the playoffs in 2022 and 2023. Not only did Gambhir lead KKR to another IPL championship in 2024 but he was also persuaded by the BCCI to take on one of the most prestigious jobs in the world—the head coach of the Indian national cricket team—which he assumed from Rahul Dravid in July 2024. This tells you that successful teams do recognize the value of a leader with a crystal clear vision for success.

Once the dream is clear, the next step is to get the right people on the bus, as Jim Collins says in his book *Built to Last*. You need to have people from different backgrounds, diverse skill sets and points of view to ensure there is diversity. This diversity allows people to challenge each other, and ensures that best ideas thrive. A common mistake leaders make is hiring people who are like them and comfortable conforming to the leader's perspective. In such scenarios, contrarian views are either not heard or are assumed to be rebellious, and it is here that the team loses the chance to capture the market or take the lead. Great teams create spaces where people can express themselves without any fear or prejudice, and it is in this environment that teamwork thrives.

There is a famous story from one of the giants of the IPL, the Mumbai Indians. Despite having all the resources in the world at their disposal, Reliance Industries' IPL team couldn't win any IPL trophy from 2008 to 2013, even with icons like Sachin Tendulkar and Ricky Ponting at the helm. There was this young player in that MI dressing room who was constantly impressing everyone, not only with his batting skills but also with his innovative observations. He was not overawed by the reputation of the coaches or captains while expressing his opinions. This was the prevailing culture of Mumbai Indians in 2013 and it was no surprise that Ponting quit leadership midway and handed the reins to that young player, Rohit Sharma. In a stunning turnaround, MI won its first IPL championship in the first year of Sharma's captaincy. If anyone thought of that occurrence as merely a coincidence, then it's worth noting that under Sharma's captaincy, MI went on to win four more trophies in the next decade, making it the most successful, alongside Dhoni's Chennai Super Kings, with five trophies each.

Having a vision and creating a team is not enough. The way the vision is communicated and goals are set makes a huge difference to the team's motivation. Jim Collins, in his book, says that if you have more than three priorities, it means you do not have any. Every good company and leader are very clear in terms of what they want to achieve, and everyone in the team also understands this in the same manner as the leader does. This clarity amongst team members is the reason why their energy isn't wasted, and all of them direct their focus on the goals they have set.

Having a clear vision, getting the right people on the team, and communicating the goals to motivate people are good starting points, but what keeps them going is creation of a shared goal and reviewing it on an ongoing basis. Without this, people can fall into the trap of counting their personal achievements as a measure of their success, and in doing so, the overall goal can be lost.

If you look at the history of New Zealand's cricket team over the last three decades, they may not have won too many glittering trophies, but due to exceptional teamwork, they have often punched above their weight and carved their own niche as one of the most competitive teams of all time. Due to a technicality, Kane Williamson's Kiwi team was denied a World

Cup trophy in 2019 Cricket World Cup against England, but they won the hearts. The Kiwis didn't grumble or express bitterness, and the world acknowledged their fantastic efforts. While we often give importance to winners in sporting arenas, some of the finer lessons of teamwork and leadership come from the less-favoured teams punching above their weight. In 2021, during the inaugural World Test Championship final, the Kiwis defeated India by a margin of 0-3, humbling the mighty Indian team even on their home turf. They not only ended India's nearly 12-year dominance in Tests, marked by 18 consecutive series wins, but also demonstrated to the world that extraordinary success was possible, even without legends like Williamson in their team.

But all this means nothing without a set of values. Values describe the culture where people are aware of what constitutes acceptable behaviour and what does not. It is not just the result but also the way the result is achieved makes a huge difference. However brilliant a person is, if they do not fit within the accepted norms of the team, they must go. There is no double standard here because everyone in the team is watching and this affects the culture of the organization. In great teams, there is always a set of rules, and each member must play by those rules, no matter how great they may be. If there is any leeway, the team suffers, and it does not reach its potential.

In life, as in sport, nothing significant is achieved alone. You always have a team that works towards that same goal with you, putting their individual needs aside for the team's victory. That

> **IT IS NOT JUST THE RESULT BUT ALSO THE WAY THE RESULT IS ACHIEVED MAKES A HUGE DIFFERENCE**

collective victory, rather than personal achievement, is the fuel which drives the behaviour of each team member, as there is nothing more significant than the victory of the team, no matter how big the personal accomplishment may be. This is the essence of teamwork.

15

Prudence

To Be Wise Beyond Years

"LOOK AND SEE WHICH WAY THE WIND BLOWS BEFORE YOU COMMIT YOURSELF."

—AESOP, Aesop's Fables

Prudence means being careful with your choices, pausing to think and reflect, and considering consequences before taking action. A prudent person doesn't take unnecessary risks or do something which they might later regret. Prudence is a form of reasoning that allows you to carefully envision the long-term impacts of the actions you take today. A person who exercises daily might not see any immediate results, but they are being prudent as they know this action will benefit their health in the long run. A person investing few hundred rupees today might not make a fortune in the short term, but their continued investment can lead to a substantial wealth over time. This, again, is a trait of a prudent person.

In the late 1980s, Sanjay Manjrekar, son of a former Indian batsman Vijay Manjrekar, was being touted as the next big thing in Mumbai cricket circles, and was expected to dominate the international cricket arena. In his first eight Test matches, Sanjay scored centuries in Barbados (this was considered a formidable achievement at that time as Barbados was the fortress of the Caribbean, and not many visiting players scored a ton there), along with a century in Karachi and a double century in Lahore. For a batsman who was being hailed as the next Sunil Gavaskar, this was almost a "Gavaskarsque" start to his Test career. However, in his next 29 matches, Sanjay Manjrekar managed just a solitary hundred and faded away from the international cricket. Far from emulating Gavaskar's success, Sanjay Manjrekar's number even lagged behind his father's.

On a tour of England in 1996, Sanjay Manjrekar saw two young Indian batsmen, Sourav Ganguly and Rahul Dravid, making terrific debuts and realized that he would never be able to make a strong comeback or cement his place ever in that Indian team. So, he decided to retire early from the game, a decision that surprised many at that point of time. However, Sanjay was being prudent. He gauged tremendous opportunities in Indian broadcasting which were just opening up as a result of India's economic liberalization policy. He ventured into commentary and soon found a niche for himself among the giants like Sunil Gavaskar and Ravi Shastri. In the decades that followed, Sanjay Manjrekar has commented on more matches than he ever played, and earned millions of dollars along the way by staying associated to the game he loved. Despite his not-so-great career as a cricketer, Sanjay Manjrekar was able to rise above the unfulfilled personal ambition. Today, he has millions of followers on social media and is a credible voice as an expert in cricket.

In sports, as in life, taking a small step in the right direction can bring great rewards, while a wrong step can result in dreadful consequences. But why it is difficult for us to take that right step, even though we know it is the prudent thing to do, and get swayed by our temptations? That delicious sweet on the plate or our favourite pastry looks quite tempting and we succumb to it, even when we know that it will cause weight gain. Sometimes our emotions, like greed or fear, take over our rational thinking, and we do things which we regret later.

Let us share the story of S. Sreesanth, the former India pace bowler from Kerala. The right-arm pacer played for India for the first time in 2006, and by 2007, he was a part of MS Dhoni's T20 World Cup-winning squad in South Africa. He was also a part of the 2011 ODI World Cup-winning squad as well. In just five years with the Indian team, Sreesanth saw several highs that only a few could imagine in their entire career. And then it all vanished slowly. One bad move led to another, and his fall was as spectacular as was his rise.

In the inaugural IPL season of 2008, Sreesanth had a spat with Harbhajan Singh, who slapped him after a match because Sreesanth had apparently provoked him with some nasty comments. His tendency to invite controversies with his actions on and off the field continued, but it hit a point of no return when he was found to be among the three Rajasthan

Royals players arrested in May 2013, along with Ajit Chandila and Ankeet Chavan, for allegedly fulfilling promises made to the bookmakers in the IPL. Soon, the BCCI's disciplinary committee found him guilty of spot-fixing and subsequently he was banned from the sport for life. Although he did make a comeback in domestic cricket later and started working as commentator for *Star Sports,* the ghost of the match-fixing scandal never left him completely. In 2023, he alleged that his former teammate Gautam Gambhir had humiliated him by calling him a fixer. Overall in his career, Sreesanth managed to play 90 international games for his country, but he had the potential of playing at least 300 and become one of India's greatest fast bowlers. However, lack of prudence and guidance cost him dearly, and he remained one of those "what-if" stories of Indian cricket.

Sometimes people become prudent with experience. It is said, "Once bitten, twice shy." A misdeed or misadventure teaches us lessons that become our guiding light for future. We take care not to fall into the trap of doing something wrong.

Another quality of prudent people is their open-mindedness. They are not stuck to one point of view. They are ready to evaluate and weigh multiple options before taking a decision. This quality allows them to weigh the pros and cons of a particular decision, and predict the future far more accurately in comparison to people who act in blind faith. Prudent people don't jump to conclusions quickly or get

A MISDEED OR MISADVENTURE TEACHES US LESSONS THAT BECOME OUR GUIDING LIGHT FOR FUTURE

swayed by others' opinions and persuasions. They can evaluate a situation quickly and act according to their critical thinking. They may take advice from others, be open to suggestions, but will not act unless they form their opinion based on all the inputs they receive.

Prudence also comes to those who pause and look at the problem from a different perspective and realize that an alternate course of action can give them better results. Normally, people don't save enough for their retirement because it feels too distant. One is not able to foresee the future accurately, and hence not inclined towards doing anything about it in the present. Prudent people do the opposite; they are able to foresee that future and take action, which ensures them a better tomorrow.

A recent experiment on age-progression technology showed that people who were shown a realistic, computer-generated image of their older selves exhibited increased tendency to sacrifice immediate rewards for a better tomorrow. They realized that the future was evident and there was no escape from that feeling that if something is not done today, tomorrow could be horrible. Another experiment by Neil Lewis and Daphna Oyserman found that people were more likely to save for retirement when it was framed as "10,950 days away" instead of "30 years away" (both of them being the same time period). When a person takes a pause, reframes the issue, and imagines a realistic future, their decisions become prudent. They act today for a better tomorrow, even if it requires sacrifices in the present.

During India's 2023 tour of South Africa, captain Rohit Sharma and coach Rahul Dravid were perturbed by the lack of fire among the young players for Test cricket, the ultimate format. They simply could not blame the youngsters alone, as they were aware that the young players, today, had an easier and more lucrative option of playing IPL for two months and earning a fortune. Test cricket, by contrast, was harder and less financially rewarding. Sharma and Dravid, and their chief selector Ajit Agarkar decided that something drastic had to be done to make Test cricket a priority for the next generation.

Fortunately, they found a fine listener in Jay Shah, Honorary Secretary of the BCCI and the President of the Asian Cricket Council (ACC) who agreed with the trio's suggestion that a suitable financial reward was the need of the hour. The moment India triumphed against England by 4-1 in a highly competitive Test series, Shah announced the "Test Cricket Incentive Scheme" for Senior Men's team. This was largely aimed at providing financial growth and stability to those players who prioritized red-ball cricket (Test match aspiration for India).

According to the official BCCI website, "this scheme is not only designed to encourage players to engage in the purest format of the sport but also addresses the evolving dynamics of the cricketing landscape, ensuring parity with match fees in other formats and league cricket." This was still comparatively less rewarding for many fine players as compared to their representation in a full season of the IPL, yet it was good enough to attract many who were prioritizing IPL over Test cricket. Of course, over the next few years, this prudent decision taken by the BCCI is likely to evolve further, and there could come a time when playing Test cricket for India becomes more rewarding than representing an IPL franchise. However, only time will tell the effectiveness of this decision.

Prudence is truly a virtue that enables other virtues to come into play. It is the prudence of an individual that allows them to do things which might not be enjoyable at that moment but are hugely beneficial in the long term. It is prudence that empowers a person to take steps that may seem ordinary to others, but which, oblivious to the ordinary person's beliefs, gives extraordinary results to the prudent individual.

MANAGING CHANGE

16

Gratitude

Being Thankful Even for the Smallest Gifts in Life

"IN ORDINARY LIFE, WE HARDLY REALIZE THAT WE RECEIVE A GREAT DEAL MORE THAN WE GIVE, AND THAT IT IS ONLY WITH GRATITUDE THAT LIFE BECOMES RICH."

—DIETRICH BONHOEFFER, German Lutheran pastor

Ever since Rohit Sharma took over the full-time captaincy of the national cricket team in late 2021, there has been an ongoing debate in the Indian media about whether the leadership role came a little too late for the Mumbai batsman. In the most competitive cricket league (IPL), Sharma had led with distinction by winning five trophies—an achievement only matched by the peerless MS Dhoni. Many felt that Sharma would never get India captaincy as he was on the wrong side of 30, and if there was a need for a new captain, a younger player would be groomed for that role. However, a lot of things changed dramatically in ways no one could have anticipated. Virat Kohli resigned from Test captaincy after being denied the leadership in white-ball formats (T20Is and ODIs). The BCCI had no other option but to appoint Rohit Sharma as a short-term captain.

As luck would have it, Sharma not only led India to semi-finals in the 2022 ICC Men's T20 World Cup in Australia, but also captained the World Test Championship final in June 2023 and the ODI World Cup final in November 2023, after India set a record by winning 10 consecutive matches. During the India tour of the West Indies in August 2023, before leaving for India, Sharma told me (Vimal Kumar) privately that he had already decided that he would not play in the next T20 World Cup, however, was asked to lead the Indian team in T20 World Cup, which was to be held in June 2024. During India's tour of the West Indies in August 2023, Sharma confided in me (Vimal Kumar) that he had already decided not to play in the next T20 World Cup. However, he was later asked to lead the Indian team in the tournament, which was scheduled for June 2024. As are well aware, the entire world witnessed the thrilling victory as Sharma guided India to a T20 World Cup win after a gap of 13 years. Even by a conservative estimate, by the time Sharma retires from international cricket, he will have led India in more matches than all but four captains.

On the sidelines of a Test match in Ranchi in February 2023, Sharma told me exclusively: "I am really a satisfied man. I don't think too much about future. I'm grateful to have captained India, which is a huge honour for me. There have been several great and fine candidates who never got an opportunity to lead India. It is easy to crib and complain about what should have happened, and some people keep telling me that I should have gotten the captaincy a lot earlier. But I tell them that look at the guys who were captaining before me: Dhoni and Kohli.

Can you argue that I deserved it ahead of them?"

The essence of that hour-long conversation with him was how content and grateful he was for what he had accomplished in his career, rather than dwelling on how fantastic and different it could have been, given the talent he seemingly possessed. Rohit Sharma, who debuted before Virat Kohli and was expected to be the next superstar of Indian cricket, lost his way in between but bounced back strongly at the right time before it was too late for a turnaround. He not only transformed himself as a reliable Test opener in later years but also earned plaudits for his authentic brand of leadership. A lot of good things have happened especially in his late 30s, which, according to Sharma, is because he was grateful for what he has accomplished.

"I really do not compare myself with anyone. By the time I finish my career, only Tendulkar, Dravid, Gavaskar, and Kohli would have more runs than me, but I may be among top three Indian players in terms of scoring international hundreds. Isn't that worth enough celebrating? I mean, you can always be greedy and think about what you could have done, but eventually, you realize how much kindness you have received from the Almighty," Sharma said, smiling, as he left for his team meeting.

HUMANS HAVE A UNIQUE QUALITY: THEY OFTEN DON'T NOTICE WHAT THEY HAVE UNTIL THEY LOSE IT

Humans have a unique quality: they often don't notice what they have until they lose it. It is the afterthought which allows them to see the beauty in what they possessed, however small.

We all know the famous story of King Midas, who derived greatest pleasure from gold. Thinking and dreaming about gold all day, believing if he had enough gold, he would be the happiest person on earth. So, when Dionysus, the Greek god of wine and revelry, granted him a boon, he wished for everything he touched to turn to gold. Dionysus warned him to think twice, but Midas was sure of his desire. So, when the god finally granted him the wish he asked for, Midas rejoiced. He touched everything around him, and everything he touched turned into gold. But then, when he felt hungry and tried to eat, the food turned into gold. The water he wanted to sip also turned to gold. He panicked. When his daughter ran to hug him, she, too, turned to gold upon touching him. What seemed like a blessing was now a curse, realized Midas. He pleaded with Dionysus to reverse the wish. The god obliged, and everything returned to normal. Midas, now, was a truly happy man.

As much as this story is about greed and love of materialistic things, it is also about gratitude. Gratitude means appreciating what we have, rather than fretting over what we don't. After this experience, Midas understood that there is beauty in the smallest things around him and realized how lucky he was to experience them. The thought that one is blessed brings a lot of solace to those who nurture it.

Robert Emmons, perhaps one of the most accomplished researchers on the subject of gratitude, talks about its two elements: First, it is an affirmation of the goodness around us, and second, we acknowledge that this goodness comes from someone or something else. It can be a person, a force, or something we do not even know about, and that's why gratitude becomes an extremely strong source for building relationships. You realize that others have contributed to your success, and this bond deepens your connection with all those who helped you become who you are.

If you listen to the interviews of Virender Sehwag, Yuvraj Singh, Ashish Nehra, Harbhajan Singh, and many more players, they all have attributed their success to their captain Sourav Ganguly. Similarly, the likes of Virat Kohli and Ravindra Jadeja and many others hail MS Dhoni as someone who backed them when no one else did. It is easy to brag about one's hard work, discipline, and work ethic, which, of course, are important aspects of a successful life, but to acknowledge the people who helped you in critical hours is the essence of gratitude. Very few successful people do this sincerely and publicly.

No wonder the famous social scientist, George Simmel, calls gratitude as "the moral memory of the mankind." The way members of a tribe helped each other, it would likely foster emotional bonds, giving rise to gratitude.

Why Should One Practice Gratitude?

Over the years, with the progress in positive psychology, several hundreds of research have demonstrated the positive benefits of possessing the trait of gratitude brings us.

Some of the significant findings are as follows:

Researchers like Robert Emmons and Sonja Lyubomirsky have shown that practiing gratitude has proven to be one of the most reliable methods of increasing happiness in life. Apart from making one feel happier, it also increases other positive emotions like pleasure, enthusiasm, and willingness to do good to others.

On the other hand, researchers like Alex Wood have shown that practicing gratitude reduces anxiety and depression. The reason is simple: when someone practices gratitude, a heap of negative emotions is replaced by fresh emotions of positivity and goodness; it is the conscious filling of the space vacated by negative emotions with positive ones, and in the long term, when it becomes a habit, it helps us navigate our darker days.

Studies by Emmons and his colleague Michael McCullough suggest that practicing gratitude can reduce symptoms of diseases, strengthen our immune system, and make us less bothered by aches and pains. Our bodies become more resilient, helping us fight diseases when we practice being grateful.

"To be able to play cricket again after everything I've been through is nothing short of a miracle," was Rishabh Pant's first reaction after he was declared fit to play in the IPL 2024 in mid-March. Pant had been out of cricket for nearly 16 months after a horrific car accident in December of 2022, which had scared all the cricket fans that he may never be able to play again. In an interview with *Star Sports*, the Indian wicketkeeper revealed how his perspective on life changed dramatically after that accident.

When asked if his life changed for better after that accident, he said, "It is hard for me to say if everything around me has become more positive or even negative. However, I've gained a fresh perspective on how I view my life now. Something I value today is enjoying my life to the fullest and this includes the smallest of things that we often ignore in our routine. Everyone today is hustling and working extremely hard to achieve something special, but we have forgotten to enjoy the little things which give us joy every single day. Especially after my accident, I have found happiness in even being able to brush my teeth every day or sitting under the sun. While trying to achieve our goals, it seems like we've taken the regular things in life for granted. My biggest realization is that feeling blessed every day is also a blessing, and that's the mindset I've adopted since my setback, and being able to enjoy every moment which comes my way is something I take with me," explained the Delhi Capitals cricket captain philosophically.

Practicing gratitude also helps foster good relationships. One of the key elements of having a grateful mind is sincerely acknowledging the contributions of others towards your success. It brings a sense of togetherness. Sara Algoe, a psychologist at the University of North Carolina, has established in her research that when partners express gratitude to each other, they become far more satisfied than they would in the absence of this expressed gratitude. It helps us bring people together, and when two people work in sync, the partnership always delivers greater results.

People who practice gratitude also forgive others for their mistakes. Fred Ruskin, director of the Stanford University Forgiveness Projects, in one of his famous talks vividly explains that forgiveness requires gratitude. Those who practice gratitude understand that there are people who are inclined towards helping one another, there are also those who may act negatively towards one another. In this scenario, grateful individuals try to empathize and understand why the person would have behaved in a certain way, and they try to see if there is another way to still see a positive side to that behaviour. This is certainly a high-level thinking, but it helps, and this is all the more reason to practice gratitude.

While gratitude is often understood to be practiced in personal lives, it is equally important in professional world. Why? Because it allows us to believe that by working with others, we are a part of something bigger, and this helps us meet the higher psychological need of finding meaning and purpose. For instance, workers building a wall may look at their work as a simple construction assignment that they are getting paid for. But when they become aware that they are a part of a larger mission—such as, helping build a hospital on that construction site—it brings a sense of meaning to everyone involved. That they all got this opportunity to work together is a reason for their gratitude.

Gratitude also goes hand-in-hand with the amount of recognition one provides to others, especially their team members. When we can see the smallest impact made by a team member and take a moment to appreciate their effort and the impact it has made on the entire team, it fills the person with pride. They return with even more energy to make an impact, going beyond their call of duty to help others. This positive cycle happens because someone took time to pause and appreciate their work.

What can a leader do to enhance their team members' sense of worth?

1. **Understand the real power of a 'thank you':** When you are truly looking around and find different people doing what they should be doing to make the team succeed, a heartfelt 'thank you' goes a long way in fostering trust and appreciation. A great leader will always find ways to show his gratitude to the team members, helping them believe that their work is being seen, acknowledged, and appreciated by the leader. This, in turn, fuels their motivation.

2. **Recognize small but significant contributions:** In a Formula 1 pit spot, at least 20 mechanics are deployed to perform a series of tasks once the race car pulls in. They perform tasks like changing tyres in a matter of 2-3 seconds. They may have a small role to play, but it is a crucial one, as even one small mistake can cause the team to lose. While it's great to rejoice and appreciate the driver who wins, a sense of appreciation and gratitude should also go to the small contributors who consistently work in the background to ensure the team's success.

   Going back to cricket, the Indian cricket team often features several superstar players, along with up-and-coming sensations and some journeymen players. The backroom staff rarely gets noticed. Unless there's someone like Rahul Dravid, a legendary player in his own right, who makes sure to do so. During India's outstanding campaign in 2023 ODI ICC Cricket World Cup, social media and traditional media were surprised by the sudden attention given to the fielding coach T Dilip. His is an incredible story to share—a former math teacher, who never played cricket professionally, made it to the Indian team through hard work and passion. When Dravid took over as the head coach of the Indian team in late 2021, he picked Dilip as fielding coach, along with Paras Mhambrey as bowling coach, and retained Vikram Rathour as team's batting coach. While Mhambrey and Rathour were already colossal figures in domestic Indian cricket, only a few knew of Dilip. As the head of National Cricket Academy in Bengaluru (prior to his appointment as India's head coach), Dravid had worked with Dilip and was impressed with his skill set.

During the 2023 Cricket World Cup, Dilip proposed the idea of rewarding a fielder after every match, and he suggested that the captain or coach should present the award. The Indian team management, however, decided that it should be done by Dilip himself, as it was his idea. The fielding coach hesitated because he had never received such attention before, but he was convinced by his entire team, including Dravid, that he was the right man for that job. After every match, Dilip used interesting ideas and speeches each time he went on stage to announce the 'best fielder' of the match. This practice became a sensation on social media as well as traditional media, making Dilip a well-known figure among cricket fans. His small contributions and work were finally acknowledged.

3. **Create a culture of appreciation:** Recognition should not come only from the people at the top. In a truly great team, everyone is appreciative of each other's work because they know without the other person the team will falter. NASA might have sent two astronauts to the moon, but there were thousands who worked behind the scenes to

make this historical feat happen. Keeping everyone engaged by recognizing their efforts towards the main goal should not be the aim of just one person, it should be a part of the culture where everyone acknowledges one another for their work with a sense of gratitude. When gratitude and recognition become a part of a team's DNA, we get to see true magic in the form of great results.

17

Integrity

Doing the Right Thing, Even When No One Is Watching

"IN LOOKING FOR PEOPLE TO HIRE, LOOK FOR THREE QUALITIES: INTEGRITY, INTELLIGENCE, AND ENERGY. AND IF THEY DON'T HAVE THE FIRST ONE, THE OTHER TWO WILL KILL YOU."

—WARREN BUFFET, American businessman and investor

Winning is important in life, and everyone wants to win. In the corporate world, the desire to win is even more pronounced. Sometimes, a "whatever it takes" attitude engulfs leaders, leading them to do things that are morally and ethically wrong.

Who has captained India the most times in international cricket after MS Dhoni? Virat Kohli? Sourav Ganguly? Or Kapil Dev? These are the obvious names that come to mind. However, the surprising answer is Mohammad Azharuddin. Not just that, the former India captain is also among the top 10 all-time highest run-scorers from the country in international cricket across all formats. In fact, Azhar has more international runs than legends like Sunil Gavaskar or even a modern-day sensation Yuvraj Singh. And yet, Azhar is rarely spoken about with warmth, grace, or the respect which is usually reserved for a great player.

There is no shred of doubt that Azhar's performance with the bat made him one of the India's greatest batsman and, statistically speaking, one of its finest captains, even if not celebrated for his tactical acumen or strategic thinking. So, why he did not receive the recognition he deserved? The answer is not too hard to find. More than his cricketing accomplishments, the defining phase of his career became the disgraceful revelation of his involvement in match-fixing.

South African captain Hansie Cronje, in his confession of match-fixing, indicated that Azharuddin had introduced him to some notorious bookies. It is all well-documented that how India's premier investigating agency, the Central Bureau of Investigation (CBI), conducted a thorough investigation and later published a damning report which subsequently debarred Azharuddin from any meaningful cricket activities. The Board of Control for Cricket in India (BCCI) then banned him from cricket for life in 2000, following the findings of the CBI report. Despite entering politics and becoming a Member of Parliament in 2009, Azhar faded from public memory. A decade later, a movie made on his life failed miserably to rebuild his lost glory. Lack of integrity proved enormously damaging for Azhar. This sums up the story of how a legend's career collapsed due to a single act of dishonesty.

Integrity is about doing the right thing every time and in every situation, whether or not someone is watching. It is about being morally upright and taking a stance even when it means suffering an immediate loss. Restraining your urge to cheat, not stealing office supplies that don't belong to you, not suppressing facts when you are required to be truthful—these are some examples of upholding the integrity in one's daily life. Our integrity is tested not only in important scenarios but also in several small ones we face on a daily basis.

INTEGRITY IS ABOUT DOING THE RIGHT THING EVERY TIME AND IN EVERY SITUATION, WHETHER OR NOT SOMEONE IS WATCHING

Pointing a finger at someone and determining whether they acted with integrity or not is difficult on two counts. First, humans possess a remarkable ability to rationalize their actions. For every act that may take us away from our act of integrity, a person can provide several explanations. For example, a student caught cheating in an exam might say: "Everyone else was doing it," or "I've never done it before, this was the first time," or, "Other students asked me to show my paper and, in exchange, I asked them to show theirs." The justifications are endless. What's important to note is that for every action we take, there is an explanation or justification (in this context) which we offer ourselves, and continue doing things we know we should not be doing.

In an emotional appeal in Southwark Crown Court in London in November 2011, former Pakistani pacer Mohammad Amir said: "I want to apologize to all in Pakistan and to everyone for whom cricket is important. I did the wrong thing. I was trapped because of my stupidity. I panicked." One of the most talented pace bowlers of his generation, Amir was infamously caught for his involvement in spot-fixing in a *News of the World* expose. Amir, along with his fellow pacer Mohammad Asif, had carried out specific on-field actions, including bowling no-balls at pre-determined times, during the Lord's Test against England (in 2008) under the instructions and involvement of their captain, Salman Butt. This was done on the orders of a bookie. Initially, they all denied the allegations offering lame excuses like "I was trapped" even in the face of video recordings.

Another challenge in judging the conduct of a person with integrity is that it is subjective in nature. What seems like an act of integrity to one person might be seen as dishonest behaviour to another. In some cultures, giving gifts for business purposes is normal, while in other cultures, it is seen as a corrupt practice. For some, exaggerating the benefits of a product or a service is a necessary to boost the sales, but for others, being discreet about the information you give out at the time of selling is the right thing to do. In the end, integrity is defined by each individual's perspective, making it difficult to agree on a universal understanding of this term.

Combining the human tendency to rationalize their actions with the difficulty in defining integrity leaves us on sticky wicket. Trying to ensure it solely through policies, processes, and audits is not feasible.

Match fixing corruption crept into cricket in the late 1980s and prospered in the 1990s. Several cricketers were banned for life and ostracized from the community, yet some players never seemed to learn from the past. The likes of Sanath Jayasuriya (former Sri Lankan captain and an all-time great), Marlon Samuels (caught not once but twice!), Shakib Al Hasan (former Bangladesh captain and another all-time great), and many others were disgraced by bans imposed from cricket's supreme body, the ICC, in recent years. Before someone offers a lazy justification that the corrupt practices were happening only in the subcontinent or the Caribbean, they must not forget the cases of all-rounder Chris Cairns and batter and occasional wicketkeeper Lou Vincent from New Zealand. Human greed knows no race or religion, and anyone can succumb to temptation if they are not vigilant enough or unaware of dangerous consequences.

What we need is a culture where integrity is not only revered but also demonstrated by everyone in their daily dealings. And for that to happen, a few things are necessary.

1. **Leaders set the course:** When Sourav Ganguly took over the captaincy in early 2000s, following the match-fixing scandal in India that had several players indicted (besides former skipper Azharuddin), he and his teammates took an 'oath' that they would never speak to the likes of Ajay Jadeja, Manoj Prabhakar, Ajay Sharma, or Nayan Mongia again. Rahul Dravid famously refused to acknowledge Jadeja's presence in the lobby of Colombo's Taj Samudra Hotel when the latter came for an NDTV cricket assignment in 2006. Similarly, Javagal Srinath, Anil Kumble, and Sachin Tendulkar agreed that they would never share a stage with the disgraced cricketer again. This set a high bar for morality in Indian cricket, which remained in place until the Sreesanth incident happened in the IPL. Only in the last few years has Tendulkar publicly begun talking to or meeting with Azhar and Jadeja, his former teammates.

2. **Be explicit about acceptable behaviour:** Since it is difficult to define integrity for everyone, it's important for a team or an organization to explicitly define acceptable behaviour. There should be no ambiguity in how it is

understood by every member of the team or organization. If someone demonstrates it, they should be rewarded. And if there is a departure from what is agreed by the team, the admonishment should also be clearly communicated and enforced.

3. **There is no such thing as over-communication:** Just being explicit about what is acceptable behaviour may not be enough. Constant reminders are equally important. Not only must the leader continually emphasize about integrity at every available opportunity but also encourage team members to talk about it regularly. Instilling integrity in the team's culture is like trying to change consumer behaviour through TV advertisements. If you air it only once, it does not make any impact. For it to make a lasting impression, repetition plays a crucial role.

4. **Create an environment where people can speak up:** Often, well-intended thoughts and ideas don't take shape on the ground because people lack the courage to stand up and call out a misdeed by the other person. This is either because of fear of consequences or being labelled as complainers. If your team members have even an iota of such a feeling, it means they don't find themselves in a safe environment where they can speak their mind, voice their concerns, and uphold the culture that is vital to the organization. In a healthy team or organization, people are encouraged to speak up, point out anomalies, and are rewarded for upholding ethical standards. People thrive in such environments.

5. **Actions speak louder than words:** Thousands of words on integrity and ethical behaviour won't mean anything if no action is taken against those who are caught violating

these principles. High performers and superstars sometimes manage to get away with their unethical behaviour because of the value they bring on table, and this damages the overall culture.

If a Pakistani player is caught in match-fixing or spot-fixing, there is no shock value in that news anymore. Over the past three decades, corruption in cricket has become so rampant in Pakistan that players are often viewed with suspicion. The main reason for this is the Pakistan Cricket Board's (PCB) failure to adequately punish the greats like Wasim Akram and Waqar Younis, who were implicated in the Justice Qayyum report.

In the report that was published in May 2000, Justice Qayyum not only had banned former Pakistani captain Salim Malik but had also reprimanded Wasim Akram, Mushtaq Ahmed, Waqar Younis, Inzamam-ul-Haq, Akram Raza, and Saeed Anwar with monetary fines. In fact, Justice Qayyum had clearly warned of the dangers if these players were allowed to remain involved in cricket, directly or indirectly. However, most of these players continued to be a part of the mainstream cricket community through their careers in broadcasting or coaching. It set a wrong precedent for the next generation, and the cases of Salman Butt, Mohammad Amir, Mohammad Asif, and Danish Kaneria to name a few, followed in the next decade or so.

EVERY SMALL DECISION YOU MAKE BUILDS YOUR REPUTATION, AND ONE SLIP CAN TAKE AWAY EVERYTHING YOU HAVE BUILT FOR YOURSELF

Conducting oneself with a high level of integrity is not easy. Every small decision you make builds your reputation, and one slip can take away everything you have built for yourself. Integrity is not a game where you can win with higher percentages. Leading with integrity means upholding your morals each time without any exceptions, and creating a legacy where winning is important but not at the cost of one's character and reputation. Even if you win without being honest with others and your game, somehow your conscience will tell you that this win was not worth it. So, lead with integrity, like the former Pakistani captain, Imran Khan, did in the 1970s and '80s—unlike his successors, who brought infamy to the country by being dishonest to their game and cricket fans.

18

Kindness

Seeing Yourself in Everyone and Treating Everyone with Love and Care

"A SINGLE ACT OF KINDNESS THROWS OUT ROOTS IN ALL DIRECTIONS, AND THE ROOTS SPRING UP AND MAKE NEW TREES."

—AMELIA EARHART, American aviation pioneer

Kindness is a type of behaviour that involves acts of consideration, generosity, assistance, and concern for others' well-being without expecting anything in return. What makes a great leader truly great is their understanding of others in the best possible manner and their ability to use words and actions in a way that makes people feel cared for. It requires listening without being judgmental, understanding the needs and wants of others, and striving to make them happier. In a world divided with caste, creed, community, and causes, kindness can act as the glue which holds humanity together. In real life and in sports, great leaders are known for their acts of kindness, which touches the other person so deeply that they follow that leader for life.

"Rohit Sharma is a special person, an outstanding leader with a golden heart. I saw it first-hand. I'd give my life for him on the field; that's the kind of captain he is. It's because of these qualities that he's won so many titles, including five IPLs. I pray to God that Rohit achieves even more in his career and life." This quote is translated from India's legendary spinner Ravichandran Ashwin's YouTube channel where he profusely praised his captain Rohit Sharma, not for his cricket captaincy but for his kindness and empathy towards him.

If you are unfamiliar with the backstory, let us take you back to the India-England Test series which was played in the early months of 2024. One of India's greatest bowlers of all time, Ravichandran Ashwin, had just achieved the remarkable milestone of 500 Test wickets in the third Test of the series, played in Rajkot. However, he had to leave the match midway due to his mother's ill health. According to the spinner, after getting his historic 500th wicket, he was expecting a call from his wife or father. He was a bit surprised not to hear from them, since it was almost 7 p.m. Eventually, he got to know about his mother's health condition from his wife, and was emotionally distressed.

Caught in a catch-22 situation, Ravichandran Ashwin desperately wanted to be with his mother but also felt responsible towards his teammates. His internal struggle and dilemma dissipated when Sharma, along with head coach Rahul Dravid, came into the dressing room and said, "What are you doing? You need to leave right away. Please pack your bags and go." Sharma also assigned one of his support staff, Kamlesh Jain, (the team's physiotherapist) to accompany the spinner, and kept checking in on him through Jain. This act of kindness deeply moved Ravichandran Ashwin.

"In a selfish society like ours, a person like Rohit who takes a moment to think about someone else's well-being is truly great," he said. This was one of the highest forms of praise ever given to an Indian captain. Mind you, Ravichandran Ashwin had played under fine captains, including MS Dhoni and Virat Kohli. At one point, he even said that the Indian dressing room no longer fosters friendships, players today only stick to their professional work relationships. But after this kind gesture by Rohit Sharma—who, without any hesitation, allowed his star player to leave an important match midway to tend to his ailing mother—earned tremendous respect from the spinner.

"Thinking about another person, understanding their troubles, and taking care of that ... it's a rarity to find these qualities in a person today. My respect for Rohit grew more ... I already have a lot of respect for him. If he believes in a player, he backs that player. It's not an easy thing. Even Dhoni does that. But he (Rohit) has taken 10 steps more. When it gets so personal like this, a player can even give his life on the field," said Ravichandran Ashwin, appreciating all the help that Rohit Sharma provided during the emotional rollercoaster he was going through in Rajkot. The spinner's story also underlines the fact that even the most successful and top athletes do need kindness from their surroundings.

Life, like cricket, is a team sport. You may be the best but you still need support from those around you. Kindness towards others makes them want to be good to you, because kindness is contagious. The person doing

YOU MAY BE THE BEST BUT YOU STILL NEED SUPPORT FROM THOSE AROUND YOU

the act of kindness experiences what Melanie Rudd, a professor of marketing at University of Houston, calls "Helper's High." At the same time, others who witness or receive kindness are inspired to act kindly themselves. This phenomenon is called inspired altruism, where an act of helping others and seeing others happy develops a feeling of warmth. People then not only imitate the kind act but also embrace the spirit behind it. Kindness helps one build long-lasting bonds.

So, what makes a person kind? It is the attitude towards helping others and taking effort towards it. Kindness is not about grand gestures, but tiny, small acts that make the other person feel seen and cared for. Like all good things, kindness is a behaviour which needs to be nurtured and practiced. Eventually, it becomes your second nature, and helps you spread happiness wherever you go. The best part is when others feel happier because of your kindness, you experience the 'Helper's High', which makes you happy, too.

There is a famous story about the South African anti-apartheid activist Nelson Mandela. Once, at a restaurant, he saw a man eating alone and invited him to join his table. The man trembled and could hardly move his hand properly. One of Mandela's security personnel pointed this out and said that the person could be sick. Mandela then put his arm around that man and introduced him as the jail guard of the same prison where he spent 27 years of his life. During that time, this guard did not treat Mandela well, and was expecting

LIKE ALL GOOD THINGS, KINDNESS IS A BEHAVIOUR WHICH NEEDS TO BE NURTURED AND PRACTICED

revenge from the great man. However, Mandela had long since forgiven the prison guard and greeted him with kindness, as it is not in his nature to hate or seek revenge. Once you treat others as people who need to be loved and nurtured, kindness organically follows.

In January 2019, South African captain Faf du Plessis did something remarkable. His team chose to forgive Pakistani wicketkeeper Sarfaraz Ahmed for his racially charged on-field taunt during an ODI match in Durban. Ahmed was heard on the broadcast's stump microphones making a racist remark in Urdu directed at South African player Andile Phehlukwayo. During South Africa's batting innings, Sarfraz Ahmed was caught clearly on the stump mics saying, in Urdu: *"Abey kaale, teri ammi aaj kahaan baitheen hain, hain? Kya parwa ke aaye hai aaj?"* Translated literally, it means: "Hey black guy, where's your mother sitting today? What [prayer] have you got her to say for you today?" It was so blatant that even someone unfamiliar with Urdu would get a hint that it must have been something terrible. On commentary, South African commentator Mike Haysman asked his fellow commentator Ramiz Raja, "What's he saying there, Ramiz?" The former Pakistan captain Raja replied, "It's a long sentence; difficult to translate," to save not only Sarfaraz Ahmed but his countrymen from embarrassment.

Given the sensitive history of South Africa, Ahmed's reckless remark in the heat of the moment had the potential of causing a diplomatic row. However, this was nipped in the bud by an act of kindness from South African skipper du Plessis. "We forgive him because he said sorry. He has apologized and taken responsibility for it. It is out of our hands, and ICC will have to deal with it now," said the South African skipper. This came after Ahmed had issued a general apology via Twitter the day after the incident, claiming that his comments were "not directed towards anyone in particular."

"When you come to South Africa, you have to be very careful when you make racial comments," du Plessis said. "I am sure he didn't mean it like that but he has taken responsibility and we will have to see what the outcome of that is going to be. We're not taking it lightly, but the fact that there was an immediate apology shows there is regret. We can forgive, but that doesn't mean we brush it under the table," du Plessis added demonstrating a balance between holding someone accountable and showing kindness. However, in that crowded press conference, what stood out the most was the light-hearted remark the South African skipper made to lighten the tense atmosphere. "We're a gracious team. We forgive easily. Maybe not so much when it's Australia." The mention of Australia was in a lighter vein, as cricketing teams often get hostile crowd and media attention, with even former players trying to intimidate the visiting teams with provocative words.

Another essential ingredient for being kind is treating people without any prejudice or bias. It is easier said than done, but it is extremely important. Once, on a train trip, we saw a mother neglecting her kids, paying them no attention. Our mind quickly concluded that she is such an irresponsible mother—only to realize how wrong we were in our judgment when we learned that she had just lost her husband and was returning home after the funeral. Our initial thought of her being negligent and irresponsible immediately gave way to empathy. We could see the situation more clearly because we had the full story now. Often, we jump to conclusions without understanding the context, and ending up acting in an unkind manner. This story shows that everyone has a backstory, everyone has a context in which they are operating, and we often have no clue what that backstory might be. If we don't understand someone's circumstances, we have no right to be unkind. We do need to err on the side of kindness to ensure we don't mistreat others.

One thing we have learned from great people is how they interact with others through their choice of words.

We'd like to share a personal anecdote from our own experiences with the Indian cricket team. Vimal Kumar was the only Indian journalist covering the series in the Caribbean in 2022. A simple act of kindness from India's young player, Sanju Samson, left an indelible impression on his mind. After the third ODI in Port of Spain, Kumar got a chance to interact with this star batter. When Kumar mentioned that the venue (Brian Lara Stadium in Tarouba) for the first T20I was a bit far from their current location, Samson offered to help and invited the journalist to tag along with him on the Indian team bus.

There have been countless such occasions over the last two decades with the Indian team where Vimal Kumar was on his own, or with a fellow journalist, in remote overseas locations, yet no one had ever offered such help. Of course, there is a protocol in place by the BCCI which prohibits journalists to travel with the team. Samson's offer was made not in his capacity as a star cricketer, but as a fellow human being and countryman in a foreign land. Kumar thanked Samson for this kind gesture and politely refused the offer as he could manage his travel with a local taxi. Even if the journalist had wanted to travel with them, he couldn't, as it would violate BCCI's protocols, and he didn't want to put Samson in an awkward situation with the management if they didn't oblige to his offer.

Vimal Kumar even shared his experience in a video on

his YouTube channel which garnered over half million views. Rajasthan Royals, the team Samson captains in the IPL, further posted the video on their official X (formerly Twitter) and Instagram accounts with a caption: "Winning hearts, winning at life—our Sanju."

> **YOU DO NOT HAVE TO SPEND MILLIONS OF DOLLARS TO BE KIND. KINDNESS IS INEXPENSIVE**

You do not have to spend millions of dollars to be kind. Kindness is inexpensive. It is the way you speak, the tone with which you greet others, and the interest you show in trying to help. Even a small gesture of helping a differently-abled person to cross the street, giving water to a thirsty person, surprising your neighbour with delicious food—counts. It is the intent behind the action that holds great value. At the very least, we can choose our words in ways that bring comfort to others; this costs us nothing. It is surprising why still a lot of us do not embrace kindness in daily life.

Here are three practices we believe can help us become kinder:

1. **Practice small act of kindness every day:** Instead of waiting for a grand gesture of kindness, focus on small actions that make others feel better, happier, and successful. These small acts will go a long way in strengthening your 'kindness muscle'.

2. **Read about the good things done by people around the world:** Subscribe to blogs, websites, or apps where you can read about acts of goodness by others. Research by a professor of psychology at the Stanford University, Jamil Zaki, shows that when we see goodness around us and

believe that good people are doing good things, we are more likely to do good ourselves.

3. **Encourage others to do good as a team:** The power of teamwork goes a long way in helping us feel better about ourselves. When others join you in your act of kindness, happiness multiplies. Consider setting aside a day of the month to perform random acts of kindness together as a group, and then have a free-flowing discussion about how it felt. You are likely to experience what's known as the "helper's high."

In life, what defines us is our relationships. According to the Harvard Study of Adult Development, which is one of the world's longest studies on adult life, what defines relationships is the kindness you pour into it. The more you act with generosity, altruism, and kindness, the more people are drawn towards you. In that journey, you not only feel a raw happiness inside, but you also inspire others to experience the same. With such experiences, life becomes beautiful not just for you, but for everyone around you.

So, be kind to people—today and always.

> **THE MORE YOU ACT WITH GENEROSITY, ALTRUISM, AND KINDNESS, THE MORE PEOPLE ARE DRAWN TOWARDS YOU**

19

Adaptability

Go with the Flow, Be Present in the Moment

"AND THE MOST SUCCESSFUL PEOPLE ARE THOSE WHO ACCEPT, AND ADAPT TO CONSTANT CHANGE. THIS ADAPTABILITY REQUIRES A DEGREE OF FLEXIBILITY AND HUMILITY MOST PEOPLE CAN'T MANAGE."

—PAUL LUTUS, American computer programmer

Adaptability is defined as the ability to change oneself to suit different conditions. Those who can adapt thrive and those who cannot go out of business.

Australian cricketer Steven Smith is arguably the finest Test batsman of the modern era. He played more than 100 Tests matches, which by itself is a testament to his longevity. His Test record was far better than even the likes of Virat Kohli, Joe Root, and Kane Williamson. Smith, Kohli, Root, and Williamson were considered the awesome foursome of the 2010s. Apart from Smith, all the other three were regarded as future batting greats by many experts from the very beginning.

But perhaps no one saw the potential of Smith, who would go on to become the greatest of them all. You can't blame anyone for that because Smith began his Test career in 2010 as a leg spinner who batted at number eight, a very low position for a specialist batsman. Smith, when he started, was seen as the next Shane Warne, but he could not come even close to that kind of comparison. His performance as a bowler was not remarkable. So much so that former Australian great Rodney Marsh—a man who was regarded as an astute figure when it came to identifying talented cricketers—rather bluntly observed: "When we first became selectors [in November 2011] he wasn't a good enough bowler, he wasn't a good enough batsman, but he certainly was a good enough fieldsman. All he had to do was improve his batting and bowling—a lot easier said than done."[1]

Smith transformed himself from an ordinary leg spinner to a world-class Test batter through sheer determination and adaptability. In 2010 and 2011, when he was primarily picked as a bowler, Smith played just five Test matches. But from 2013 onwards, he became a colossal figure and was hailed as one of the finest Test batters of all time.

Sometimes, our past success becomes a barrier to bringing about change. We grow complacent about the

> **SOMETIMES, OUR PAST SUCCESS BECOMES A BARRIER TO BRINGING ABOUT CHANGE**

---

[1] 2015, Daniel Brettig | December. "The Adaptable Mr Smith." Cricinfo, December 1, 2015. https://www.thecricketmonthly.com/story/940149/the-adaptable-mrsmith.

methods that made us successful, and become blind to the fact that when circumstances change, the same methods will no longer hold us in good stead.

The decline of Pakistani cricket in the last two decades clearly illustrates this. The same can be seen in the downfall of the West Indies cricket team, which once ruled the world. The West Indies made it to three consecutive ODI Cricket World Cup finals, winning the tournaments on two of those occasions in 1975 and 1979. But, after 1983, they never qualified for an ODI World Cup final again. Such became their abysmal state that they could not even qualify for the 2023 World Cup in India! Both teams may have believed that their natural reserves of world-class fast bowlers and batters would never dry up. They failed to adapt to the demands of modernization in international cricket.

Teams that adapted to new technologies and gave paramount importance to fitness standards, marched ahead. On the other hand, lack of attention to these two key aspects led to the sad decline of cricketing infrastructure in Pakistan and the West Indies. On occasion, both teams do surprise their opponents with miraculous performances. However, the aura of greatness that was once associated with them in the 1980s and 1990s has now vanished.

In contrast to resting on one's laurels, an insatiable curiosity to learn and innovate prepares leaders to adapt well to different situations.

Rahul Dravid's journey—as a player who went on to become the captain and then the head coach years after retirement—is an example of a man who continually reinvented himself to become a long-term success. When Dravid started his career, he wasn't considered good enough as a batsman in the ODI format, and was dropped from the team. However, his captain, Sourav Ganguly, was convinced that Dravid could adapt to new challenges, and asked him to become the wicketkeeper—a dual role that he wasn't used to until then. With this, Dravid cemented his position in the playing eleven. Dravid did not let his ego get the better of him, and adapted himself to the team's need for a wicketkeeper-batsman. Of course, he didn't captain the side for very long period and his stint was mainly remembered for the controversies his coach Greg Chappell created around the team. Nevertheless, Dravid still managed to leave an imprint with Test series wins in the West Indies in 2006 and in England in 2007.

After retirement, Dravid continued to evolve in his roles as a mentor and director with the Delhi Daredevils (now Delhi Capitals) and the Rajasthan Royals in the Indian Premier League. He later became the India Under-19 coach and eventually graduated to the role of the head coach for the national men's team. He did not rest on his laurels as an iconic cricketer. Nor did he settle for the relatively easier option of commentary box. He continued to be a student of the game.

Another hallmark of adaptable people and companies is their growth-oriented mindset. When they are stuck with a problem, they take it as an opportunity to evolve and grow.

To develop this adaptability, we need resilience. When tough times come, we do our best to survive. Sometimes we fail, and sometimes we overcome the

ANOTHER HALLMARK OF ADAPTABLE PEOPLE AND COMPANIES IS THEIR GROWTH-ORIENTED MINDSET

challenging situation through resilience. Even when we cannot face up to challenges, we cannot give up, because actual defeat lies in giving up. By the time we get back up on our feet after falling and fight with renewed vigour, we are in the game. This resilience helps build adaptability because when you face such situations in life, you are ready for more. You do not get afraid of what life has in store for you, because you know that whatever it may be, you will take it positively and turn it to your advantage.

In today's volatile world, one cannot predict what will happen next. One cannot make ironclad plans for the next five or ten years. It is important to be ready to face any challenge. Building a mindset of adaptability prepares us to do exactly that. Those who do not adapt to the changing times risk facing rapid extinction, whether in life or in business.

So, change with the change, before the change changes you.

20

Perspective

Looking Beyond the Obvious

Let me start this chapter with a slightly different example. Imagine someone who, after finishing a day's work, watches a few slum kids playing football with a broken bucket. Normally, people would ignore them and move on. But a sports teacher with a unique perspective saw them in a different light. When he saw a group of underprivileged kids playing football, he realized how much they loved the sport. More importantly, he realized that by staying on the field, they were not falling prey to bad habits that would hinder their growth as they hailed from disadvantaged backgrounds. He looked at football as a vehicle to change the lives of these kids. That's how Vijay Barse, a sports teacher from a Nagpur college, started an initiative called *zopadpatti* (slum) football, which later metamorphosed into an organization named Slum Soccer. In an interview to *The Indian Express*, Barse said, "I am a sports teacher, but I am not promoting the development of football; I am promoting development through football." This is the power of perspective. It allows you to look at the same situation differently and bring an entirely new dimension into the world.

The word 'perspective' is rooted in the Latin word 'perspicere', which means "to look closely". When you have perspective, you do not miss the forest for the trees. You have the capability to look beyond the mundane workings of the world. Different people can have different perspectives depending on their backgrounds, beliefs, and experiences.

We all know the story of five blind men and the elephant. When each of them described the part of the elephant that they touched, they explained only their own perspective. In real life, too, we sometimes perceive things only based on our own understanding and then shut ourselves from hearing other people's perspectives. If we do that, we ensure that we neither grow nor are we ready to tackle the challenges that life throws at us.

Over the past few decades, winning a Test series in Australia has been considered as the toughest challenge not only for Indian cricket teams but also for other teams from the subcontinent. India won its first-ever Test series in Australia in 2018-19 under Virat Kohli's captaincy. When India toured Australia again in the 2020-21 season, an encore was least expected, especially after the horrendous showing in the very first match of the series, when India got bundled out for a mere 36 runs in the first innings in Adelaide. The team had already been under enormous pressure because prior to the matches, they had been cooped up in a bio-bubble for many weeks due to the COVID-19 pandemic. The defeat in the first match would certainly have demoralized the players' spirits. Moreover, the sudden departure of the Indian captain Virat Kohli (he went on paternity leave after the first Test for the birth of his first child) may have led everyone to write off any chances of India's comeback in the series.

That was not all. India was ravaged by so many injuries that none of the five top bowlers on the tour—Jasprit Bumrah, Mohammed Shami, Umesh Yadav, Ravichandran Ashwin, and Ravindra Jadeja—were available for the final game in Brisbane. Forget winning, even getting 11 fit players for the match was a big challenge.

When the last game at the Gabba in Brisbane began, India's bowlers had cumulatively taken only 13 wickets in their careers. Contrast that with the Australian bowling attack which consisted of Pat Cummins, Josh Hazlewood, Mitchell Starc, and Nathan Lyon, who had collectively taken 1,013 wickets between them. Moreover, the Gabba was a fortress for the hosts as they had never lost a Test at there since 1988. And yet, India won! They not only won the game but won the series by a margin of 2-1. This victory was perhaps the greatest ever in the annals of Indian cricket.

As shared in the earlier chapter, after the win, stand-in captain Ajinkya Rahane didn't give any memorable quotes on the comeback. Rahane mentioned how he told his teammates to accept this defeat and move on. He also mentioned that there was no point going in depth and thinking about it because the [next Test] match was immediately starting in three days. His only message to his team was: "It happened in one hour. They [Australia] played good cricket. Such things happen once in a century. The faster we accept this and move on, it is good for us."

Rahane simply had a different perspective on the humiliating loss in the first game. He didn't resort to a dramatic pep talk to motivate his players. He just did something which looks simple at first, but is, in fact, the hardest thing to do—to change someone's perspective of a tough situation. "It is a good opportunity for us to stay and play as one. Whatever the result, especially after the Melbourne Test or at the end of the Test series, does not matter. Outcome is the last thing. All I wanted was that we should come together and play as one, that was my priority," Rahane had told *Sakal,* a leading Marathi daily, after the win. This exemplifies how we, too, can look at seemingly adverse situations through a different lens and turn things around when very few can imagine a comeback.

Life is often shaped by how you perceive things, and how you react to them. Sometimes, if your reaction is negative, it can send you down a negative spiral. On the other hand, if you look at things from a positive perspective, you can build something that can bring about a change.

Your ability to deal with people who have different perspectives has an impact on the way you connect with others—how you handle relationships, how you handle your problems in life and, most importantly, how do you handle the surprises that life throws at you. Looking at your problems from a different perspective also allows you to find solutions that were not visible earlier.

> **LIFE IS OFTEN SHAPED BY HOW YOU PERCEIVE THINGS, AND HOW YOU REACT TO THEM**

Once a person, exasperated by heavy traffic, saw another person in the same traffic smiling, singing, and being happy. When the latter was asked about the secret behind his cheerful disposition, he provided a different perspective to the person stuck in the same situation. He said, "When I am in traffic, I know I am going to be late. So, instead of complaining about things that I can't change, I try to do things that are in my control. See, when I am stuck in traffic, I have some time for myself. I can either waste my time sitting and regretting my bad luck, or find a new way to add value to myself. I looked at my audiobooks and said to myself—Wow, if there is more traffic, I can finish a large part of the book today. If the delay is longer than I expected, it is even better, because it gives me the opportunity to finish a book in one sitting. I get to listen to amazing authors, which would have been difficult if it not were for the traffic."

Both faced the same traffic, but they had unique perspectives. That was the reason why both experienced different emotions while in traffic. Terrific, isn't it?

One of the best ways to change your perspective in life is to find ways to help others. Those who need your help indirectly remind you that you are in a better position than them in some way. Sometimes, we fret over a missed promotion or a bonus that did not materialize. We lament that we were unlucky to not have clinched some deal or not being able to buy some car. But in these moments, we forget that there

ONE OF THE BEST WAYS TO CHANGE YOUR PERSPECTIVE IN LIFE IS TO FIND WAYS TO HELP OTHERS

are so many things that we own, which others cannot even dream of.

There was this young executive who always felt that life had not dealt good cards to him in comparison to others in his close circle. But one day, when he went to meet his ailing uncle in the hospital, he saw a patient who had forgotten how to swallow after a brain surgery. That was when it hit him that while he was fretting about deals, bonuses, and cars, there were people who could not even swallow food, something which he never even thought would be a problem for anyone. That moment changed his perspective towards life. He started being grateful for all the little things he had in life. In fact, even being able to get up in the morning and stand on his own feet started giving him happiness.

Life, indeed, is about how we perceive things and develop perspectives. It's all in the mind. The one who can train their mind to see the same thing from different points of views can claim to have truly arrived in life.

That, indeed, is the perspective that matters.

Afterword

They say that life is beautiful, but there is a catch: it doesn't become beautiful by itself. One needs to make it beautiful. You need to build a mindset that allows you to look at situations in ways that bring out the best outcomes, irrespective of what was presented to you. Therein lies the beauty of life. What we mean is, you must work towards making life beautiful. Like all things valuable, you have to work hard towards building a life that can truly be called a fulfilling life.

But where to start? How do you find the guidance to work towards a direction that leads you to your dreams? This is the question we aimed to answer through this book. We didn't want to be preachy or offer only theoretical concepts; instead, we wanted you to understand the nuances of creating a fulfilling life from real-life situations. And what better than presenting exciting, memorable, and life-defining stories from the cricketing world? Along the way, we have also shared some other examples drawn from life as both life and cricket involve people, rules, and a shared pursuit of victory.

There's a popular saying: 'You need to change first before changing the world,' and it's true. Without having your inner victory in place, you can't dream of winning in the outside world. That's why the first half of this book is dedicated to managing self.

Through the examples from the cricket field, we demonstrated how players with positive outlooks emerged as winners because nothing could deter their positive mind and stop them from trying for the glory. Positivity makes people hopeful, and that's the second character trait we discussed in detail in our second chapter. Being hopeful is antithesis of the negativity that surrounds us. It prevents us from not giving up.

In our third chapter, we discussed the concept of resilience in detail and shared numerous cricketing examples of players who made inspiring comebacks when no one thought they had a chance. How does one build resilience? By being consistent in one's behaviour, being disciplined, and ensuring that they are not distracted from their path of building good habits.

The lives of all great people teach us that the one thing that set them apart from others was their discipline. Our chapter on discipline not only defines and simplifies the term but also breaks it down to different steps for those who wish to learn and implement it in their lives.

We have also touched upon another virtue—grit, defined as not giving up on your goals despite obstacles and hardships. One demonstrates perseverance and passion for their goals and are determined to stay the course despite obstacles.

Once victory over self is achieved, we move towards managing others. Winning others starts with cultivating empathy—the ability to put oneself in the shoes of others and feel as they feel. It's about looking at a situation from other person's perspective rather than being judgmental or trying to force your view onto others. No two people in this world are similar. Everyone has a worldview of their own; and when someone tries to impose that worldview on the others, that's when conflict takes place. In this context, empathy becomes a crucial quality of a leader. Rather than pushing your worldview on others, understanding the context of a person's situation and providing them with the best solution for their needs builds trust.

We have shown this through examples of leaders like MS Dhoni and Rohit Sharma, who understand the situations of their players, empathize with them, and give them the space they need. That's what has helped players like Ravindra Jadeja, Ishant Sharma, and Surya Kumar Yadav to thrive on the cricket field. In fact, empathy is the starting point in understanding others. It allows one to be humane, considerate, and open to connecting with others. Once you practice empathy, your worldview changes, and you begin relating to perspectives that make you more considerate towards others' situations. This also enables you to develop emotional intelligence, which we have discussed in detail in the seventh chapter of this section. Emotional intelligence is nothing more than tuning into others' emotional frequencies. For this to happen, we need to understand, recognize, and regulate our emotions to begin with, and then later tune into emotions of others.

A good mix of emotion and reason is what makes life beautiful. This is why understanding and acknowledging one's emotional state is the first step towards building a great level of emotional intelligence in life. In this chapter, we talked about Sachin Tendulkar, Virat Kohli, and Rishabh Pant who exemplify this trait despite suffering major personal losses. When you have someone with great emotional intelligence, it becomes easier for them to tune into others' emotion. When this happens, the other person is willing to give everything to that person. That is the power of cultivating emotional intelligence. Combined with empathy, this intelligence brings others closer to you and helps you in achieving your goals.

Trust is, perhaps, a firm belief that someone is good, honest, and will never do things to harm you.

Once you have empathy, emotional intelligence, and trust, the next important trait to have is courage—the courage to be true to yourself, the courage to be truthful, and the courage to stand up for yourself and others. That's the hallmark of a true leader. The difference between an ordinary person and a leader is courage. While others might back themselves, true leaders have the courage to back others selflessly. This quality draws others close to them.

Finally, what makes others fall in love with you is humility. It is such an understated quality in the modern world, though it has only recently gained attention in leadership discussions. A leader who is humble understands that without staying grounded, it is difficult to win others over to an extent that they are willing to go to any length to ensure your success.

Thus, in the second section of our book, we explained the character traits that enable individuals to win others over and manage relationships with others in a way that they build deep connections and are available for each other whenever required. It all starts with empathy, which allows trust to build up and that trust makes you courageous as you can take decisions, which otherwise you wouldn't have taken.

After working on yourself and others, the next part is where the action begins. When you have a goal in life, whether in sports or business, you need a team. You can't achieve everything alone. In any team sport, everyone has a role to play, and when a team wins or loses, it is because of how each member of the team operates. In this third section, we explained the character traits that help leaders build teams and create success through them.

At the beginning of any success, what is required is a vision. A leader is someone who is responsible for a better tomorrow. They are someone who can foresee what others can't anticipate. Not only do they have the ability to look into the future, but they are also able to take actions today that shape the future.

While vision is essential, it needs to be translated into action. These actions form a part of the decisions a leader must make while implementing strategies. Here, the leader is supported by data, patterns, analysis, information, and suggestions. Based on these, a leader makes a decision. This is where judgment comes into picture, which we have explained in detail in chapter 12. Judgment—the ability to combine personal qualities with relevant knowledge and experience to form opinions and make decisions—is "the core of exemplary leadership." We have shared how right judgment ensures that a team is able to deliver the results it is built to deliver. Acting on one's judgment can lead to success or failure, and one's ability to continue with the template allows one to succeed.

Leaders are those individuals who not only continue on the path but also ensure their teams don't give up in the face of adversity; they persevere. Who can forget the perseverance of Rahul Dravid and Rohit Sharma?

A leader also understands that for the team to win, every member needs to work in synchrony. There needs to be teamwork, where everyone is aware of their roles and delivers on those expectations without fail. When we talked about this aspect, we mentioned how, at different points of time, different team members raise their hands and own up the responsibility so that the team objectives are achieved. We emphasized that a burning desire to help the team cross the line and taking immense pride in each other is the key to teamwork.

A leader also needs to demonstrate prudence in their actions. In the course of a team's journey, there are several decisions which need to be taken, and sometimes, these decisions can be difficult to swallow, but nonetheless, they need to be taken. It is at this juncture the character trait of prudence comes into picture. History offers examples where the decision taken by a leader initially looked out of context but gave results at the end of the day. It was the prudence of the leader that allowed them to look beyond the obvious and back their judgment.

Those leaders, who lead their team with lot of prudence are not only able to bring the team together but also deliver results. We have also delved into the elements of how the same can be developed by you, dear readers, so that you, too, can experience the benefits of living prudently and creating a world where success and happiness are consistently achieved.

After covering self, others, and teams, we delved into the fourth section of the book, which discusses the traits necessary to manage change and thrive. This section is important because we live in a highly dynamic world, and change is the only constant. Who saw the unprecedented and deadly outbreak of COVID-19 coming in 2020 that turned our world upside down? No one could have estimated that deadly virus halting all activities and making us realize the vulnerabilities of human life. A leader must be prepared for any eventuality. They are not only expected to manage themselves and their team but also to tackle the environment wherein they don't have any control. That is why this section of managing change is so crucial.

We have also delved deeper into the qualities or character strengths that allow a leader to mange change effectively. It all starts with a sense of gratitude.

Moving on, we understand that while having a positive mind is great in facing a difficult situation, one also needs to be true to one self and others in all situations. That character is called integrity. Integrity is about doing the right thing, every time, in every situation—whether or not someone is watching you. In a crisis, a leader is supposed to make several quick decisions that can have long-term implications on the team and team's fortune. Integrity is what guides the leader to take those decisions. It is that compass, which allows them to stick to what is right for the team and is not driven by self-interest or short-term gains. Team members often observe their leader's actions and decide whether to rally or abandon the ship. Leading with integrity may be tough, but it yields results in the long term. We explained this concept with a lot of examples and have tried to present it as simply as possible for our readers.

Another quality, which allows leaders to navigate difficult times is empathy—the ability to step into someone else's shoes and feel what they are feeling. Obviously, in a turbulent environment, most of them panic and tend to make hasty decisions which they wouldn't make otherwise. Such knee-jerk reactions are common. Leaders, however, understand this and can empathize with their team members. Instead of reacting, they respond. They try to get to the root cause of the behaviour and offer guidance that reassures their team members that their self-interest is central to the leader's approach. This creates a deep connection between the leader and the team, making team members more willing to contribute towards solving the problem at hand. That is why kindness is such an important tool with leaders. A kind leader also gains the backing of everyone they touch and can sail through any difficulty because of the collective strength of their team. It is astounding to see how much similar our lives are to the sport of cricket. The several examples from cricket we provided would surely make an impression on your minds and provide you an insight into how leaders think empathically in tough situations.

Knowing someone is good, understanding them with empathy is even better. However, the key to leadership is adaptability—the ability to accept the reality and strive to bring the best out of any situation.

Lastly, we discussed the concept of perspective—the ability to make sense of our environment, our situations, our actions, and their outcomes. A true leader has the ability to think about things on a higher plane. While the day-to-day actions may seem mundane, a leader is also aware of where the world is heading, how the team fits into that trajectory, and what role the team plays in the overall scheme of things. This quality is what we call having a perspective. A perspective can change a situation dramatically—it can make a good thing seem bad or help find goodness in a bad situation.

We saw in the last section, how a leader's ability to practice gratitude, lead with integrity, demonstrate kindness, adapt to situations, and adopt a positive perspective enables them to tackle the unknown and face any challenge that comes their way. These are life skills that, when developed, can propel leaders to the highest levels. We have tried to explain each of these concept in a lucid and simple manner, using powerful examples to leave a lasting impact on our readers. Our goal is

to help our readers become great leaders and human beings—
capable of managing themselves, guiding others, building great
teams, and facing any challenge with the strength of character
developed through the stories we have shared in this book.

Acknowledgements

Perhaps the toughest part of writing a book is expressing gratitude, as there are countless people to thank and acknowledge. Without their direct or indirect support, it would be virtually impossible to accomplish something special in life.

I owe everything to the blessings of my late grandmothers—Surdaso Devi (Dadi) and Chandmuni Devi (Nani)—and the unconditional love of my late parents, Vinayak Prasad Sah and Phool Kumari Devi. Words cannot capture what they mean to me. Emotionally, I was at my lowest when I lost my elder brother, Amarnath Gupta, during the COVID-19 pandemic. To cope with this tragic loss, I turned to writing, and I hope his soul continues to guide and bless me.

Ashish's relentless persuasion over nearly a decade and his unique idea convinced me to attempt something that's beyond cricket. Friends like Neeraj Jha, Niraj Shah (from Houston, USA) and Het Bhatt, among many others, encouraged me to spread positivity through cricket content.

A big thank you to the Board of Control for Cricket in India, with a special mention to the former secretary Jay Shah, (recently appointed as the International Cricket Council Chairman), for being generous to a freelancer like me. I would like to extend my gratitude to everyone associated with the Indian cricket team—players and support staffs alike—

who have been kind enough to share their inspirational and motivational stories with me.

The editorial team of Jaico Publishing House deserves a special mention for being extraordinarily accommodative and supportive with the deadlines on multiple occasions. Many thanks to my friend Clayton Murzello (Group Sports Editor, *Mid-Day*) who introduced me to the Jaico team.

Last, but certainly not the least, my heartfelt thanks to my soulmate Savita Singh and my lovely children Ishita and Ayan for never complaining about my absence while I was out on long tours covering cricket matches. I would also like to thank my elder brother-in-law Vijay Gupta for inspiring me with his professionalism and work ethics. Also, a special mention to my younger brother, Shailesh, for being my harshest critic at home. I am well aware that he wants me to be the best version of myself and I'm quite grateful for that.

Vimal Kumar

This book is a tribute to our friendship. Vimal and I have grown together, seen each other evolve in our respective fields, and shared a special desire to come together and create something meaningful that will remain long after we are gone. Without your friendship, Vimal, I would not have written this.

A special acknowledgement goes to my grandfather, Sri Manmohan Prasad, who instilled in me the value of pursuing knowledge from an early age. My parents, Sri Keshaw Prasad and Manju Sinha, have been constant sources of inspiration. My in-laws, late Anup and Shaileja Jayakar, have profoundly influenced my thoughts and worldview. I would also like to acknowledge my brothers, Manish and Shirish Ambasta, for shaping me into the person I am today.

This acknowledgement wouldn't be complete without a special word for Malvika, my best friend and soulmate, who continues to inspire me to give my best. My children, Anshul and Anshika, are the best and always motivate me to stay on top of my game.

The list of people I'm grateful for is long, but I feel incredibly blessed to have a family and bunch of friends who always encourage me to excel in everything I do. I love you all and feel extremely grateful to have your love in my life.

Ashish Ambasta

Sources

Section 1: Managing Self

2. Positivity

1. ESPN Digital Media Private Limited. 2024. "Harshal Patel Profile - Cricket Player India | Stats, Records, Video." ESPNcricinfo. May 5, 2024. https://www.espncricinfo. com/cricketers/harshal-patel-390481.

2. (Yanek et al. 2013) "Effect of Positive Well-Being on Incidence of Symptomatic Coronary Artery Disease." *The American Journal of Cardiology* 112 (8): 1120–25. https:// doi.org/10.1016/j.amjcard.2013.05.055.

3. Rao, K Shriniwas. 2022. "Whatever We Are Doing on the Field Right Now Is Preparation for the T20 World Cup, Says Shreyas Iyer." *The Times of India*, March 1, 2022. https://timesofindia.indiatimes.com/sports/cricket/sri-lanka-in-india/int20s-%20its-a-crime-if-you-play-a-dot-ball-shreyas-iyer/articleshow/89912453.cms.

4. ESPNcricinfo. 2021. "How Ajinkya Rahane and His Trusted Lieutenants Masterminded India's Border-Gavaskar Triumph." ESPNcricinfo, January 24, 2021. https://www.espncricinfo.com/story/aus-vs-ind-2020-21-howajinkya-%20rahane-and-his-trusted-lieutenants-masterminded-india-striumph-%201249070.

3. Resilience

1. Nair, Gokul. "'My First Series Was a Disappointment' - When Virat Kohli Addressed a Press Conference after His First Ever Test Fifty in 2011." Sportskeeda, September 16, 2024. https://www.sportskeeda.com/cricket/my-first-series-disappointment-when-virat-kohli-addressed-press-conference-first-ever-test-fifty-2011.

2. 2015, January. "The Biggest Unfulfilled Talent." Cricinfo, January 1, 2015. https://www.thecricketmonthly.com/story/816423/-the-biggest-unfulfilled-talent.

5. Grit

1. "'I Knew It Was the End of My Series; Whatever Impact I'd Have, It Had to Be Then.'" ESPNcricinfo, January 21, 2021. https://www.espncricinfo.com/story/aus-vs-ind-hanuma-vihari-i-knewit- was-the-end-of-my-series-whatever-impact-i-d-have-it-had-to-bethen- 1248681.

2. Most people fail to achieve their new year's resolution. | inc. com. Accessed October 24, 2024. https://www.inc.com/marla-tabaka/why-set-yourself-up-for-failure-ditch-new-years-resolution-do-this-instead.html.

Section 2: Managing Relationships

6. Empathy

1. Gazettemikepetroff. "Over Nearly 80 Years, Harvard Study Has Been Showing How to Live a Healthy and Happy Life." Harvard Gazette, January 11, 2024. https://news.harvard.edu/gazette/story/2017/04/over-nearly-80-years-harvard-study-has-been-showing-how-to-live-a-healthy-and-happy-life/.

8. Trust

1. Wietrak, E. and Gifford, J. (2024) Trust and psychological safety: An evidence review. Practice summary and recommendations. London: Chartered Institute of Personnel and Development. https://www.cipd.org/globalassets/media/knowledge/knowledge-hub/evidence-reviews/2024-pdfs/8542-psych-safety-trust-practice-summary.pdf

2. Jeffrey Pfeffer and Robert I. Sutton. "How Google Sold Its Engineers on Management." Harvard Business Review, May 22, 2023. https://hbr.org/2013/12/how-google-sold-its-engineers-on-management.

Section 3: Building and Managing a Team

12. Judgment

1. Kumar, Vimal. "MC Exclusive I Don't Be in Awe of Any Player: Captain Rohit Sharma's Special Motivational Class for Yashasvi Jaiswal." Moneycontrol, July 12, 2023. https://www.moneycontrol.com/news/trends/sports/mc-exclusive-i-dont-be-in-awe-of-any-player-captain-rohit-sharmas-special-motivational-class-for-yashasvi-jaiswal-10948071.html.

13. Perseverance

1. DR, Duckworth AL; Peterson C; Matthews MD; Kelly. "Grit: Perseverance and Passion for Long-Term Goals." *Journal of Personality and Social Psychology.* Accessed October 28, 2024. https://pubmed.ncbi.nlm.nih.gov/17547490/.

Section 4: Managing Change

19. Adaptability

1. 2015, Daniel Brettig | December. "The Adaptable Mr Smith." Cricinfo, December 1, 2015. https://www.thecricketmonthly.com/story/940149/the-adaptable-mrsmith.

About the Authors

VIMAL KUMAR

Vimal is a renowned cricket journalist and media personality who has worked for media houses such as *BBC, CNN-News18, IMG-TWI, India Today Group,* and *TRT World,* among others, for over two and a half decades, covering the game across continents. His refreshing brand of positive journalism has earned him the warmth and appreciation of the Indian cricket team in the last couple of years. He has written two books and runs a popular YouTube channel on cricket.

ASHISH AMBASTA

Ashish is a seasoned HR consultant and runs his own firm, HappyPlus. Prior to this, he was a consultant with global consulting firms such as Gallup, Willis Towers Watson, and Aon Hewitt, advising boards and leadership teams on building winning teams. He holds a PhD in workplace happiness and also teaches HR at various top-tier institutions.